Copyright © 2019 by Masjid Uthman (Uthman Seminary, Uthman Academy). All rights reserved. Printed in the United States of America. No part of this publication may be reproduced or distributed in any form or by any means, or stored in a database retrieval system, without the prior written permission of the publisher.

ISBN: 9781689257893

Published by:

Masjid Uthman (Uthman Seminary, Uthman Academy)
P.O. Box 2874, Glen Ellyn, IL 60138

Authors: Talha Ali, Mufti Ubaidullah Abdul Awal

بسم الله الرحمن الرحيم

In the name of Allah, most Merciful and Compassionate.

The maktab system was established by Umar (رضي الله عنه) for the education of children in the fundamental skills, values, and precepts of our Islamic civilization.

إنّ أوّل من جمع الأولاد في المكتب لتعليم القرآن عمر بن الخطاب و أ مر عامر بن عبد الله الخزاعي أن يلازمهم للتعليم و جعل رزقه من بيت المال (الفواكه الدواني)

The existence of such education is an imperative for our children's spiritual salvation and for our civilizational growth. Where public schooling systems cannot meet this need, particularly in Muslim minority countries, Muslim communities have attempted to implement independent maktab systems. In many cases, these take the shape of weekend or after school programs. Masjid Uthman (Uthman Seminary) first implemented its after school maktab system in 2015.

In July 2017, more than 20 mostly American teachers and ulema visited Sri Lanka on a maktab training and tour arranged by Mufti Ubaidullah Abdul Awal and representatives of the All Ceylon Jamiyyatul Ulama (ACJU). The ACJU developed an extensive and successful maktab system within a Muslim community facing challenges similar to those facing Muslim communities in North America.

In addition to learning what makes the ACJU maktab system effective (e.g. curriculum, teaching methodology, administration), the ulema and teachers formed an informal consultative body for future development. This included Mufti Ubaidullah Abdul Awal of Shariah Board in New York, Talha Ali of Uthman Seminary in Illinois, Qari Sohail Mangera of Al Falah Institute in Michigan, Mufti Abraar Alli of Nur e Islam Masjid in Trinidad, and Mufti Ehzaz Ajmeri of Darul Qasim in Illinois. This group continued discussing curriculum, teacher training, and other matters of maktab development in order to form a new system suited to needs of the American Muslim community. Members of this group also traveled to other countries to observe and gain insight from those countries' systems.

Masjid Uthman's existing after school maktab structure was adjusted to adopt this new system. Tools and materials to run it were developed. Deep appreciation is due to the skilled teachers, with whom Masjid Uthman is particularly blessed, and Masjid Uthman's administrative team, who eagerly supported the maktab, adopted it, continued providing feedback for its improvement, and contributed to its further development. In particular, several teachers contributed to the structure and content of the syllabi and report cards contained in this book.

This book was compiled based on the contributions above, to systematize the after school maktab, and to provide an easy-to-adopt system for other institutions in North America and beyond. Uthman Seminary's maktab has been successfully operating on this system, and it has been used by several other institutions. Hundreds of students have benefitted from it within a short span of time. We pray that more institutions can set up and improve their own maktabs by using the structure, system, and tools in this book. Training workshops are also provided to institutions who are interested in learning more.

We pray to Allah that He accepts this work as a means of our salvation in the Afterlife. Ameen.

Table of Contents

Performance Monitoring and Tracking

Attendance and Behavior
Quran Reading Rubric
Comprehensive Assessments
Trimester Report Cards (templates)

Curriculum and Syllabus

After School Islamic and Quran Studies Curriculum
Syllabus and Schedule

Student Placement

Student Placement Worksheet
Islamic Studies Placement Test (template)

Student Conduct

Student Code of Conduct
Notice of Behavioral Violation (template)

Administrative Notes

Student Notes
Meeting Notes
Student Rotational Duties
Teacher Rotational Duties
Student Medical Info
Fee Tracker (Admin Use)

Attendance and Behavior

Student Full Name (Please spell names correctly.)	Parent Name	Reg (✓)	Phone Number	Attendance Week 1 Start __/__				Week 2 Start __/__			
				M	Tu	W	Th/F	M	Tu	W	Th/F
1											
2											
3											
4											
5											
6											
7											
8											
9											
10											
11											
12											
13											
14											
15											
16											
17											

Key

Attendance
- ✓ Present
- **A** Absent
- **T** Tardy
- **S** Sick
- **L** Confirmed as Last Day (Cancel)

Behavior
- **X** Behavioral Violation
    - Not following teacher's directions and class rules
    - Making fun of or being rude to fellow students
    - Misbehaving during prayer
    - Excessive roughness during play
    - Wearing clothes to school that are unclean
- **S** Severe Behavioral Violation
    - Fighting with, beating, physically harming others
    - Using vulgar language
    - Intentionally damaging/stealing others' property
    - Insubordination, rude behavior to teacher; Cheating
    - Taunting based on race, color, language
    - Lewd and inappropriate dressing

Behavior

#									
1									
2									
3									
4									
5									
6									
7									
8									
9									
10									
11									
12									
13									
14									
15									
16									
17									

Trimester 1

Attendance and Behavior

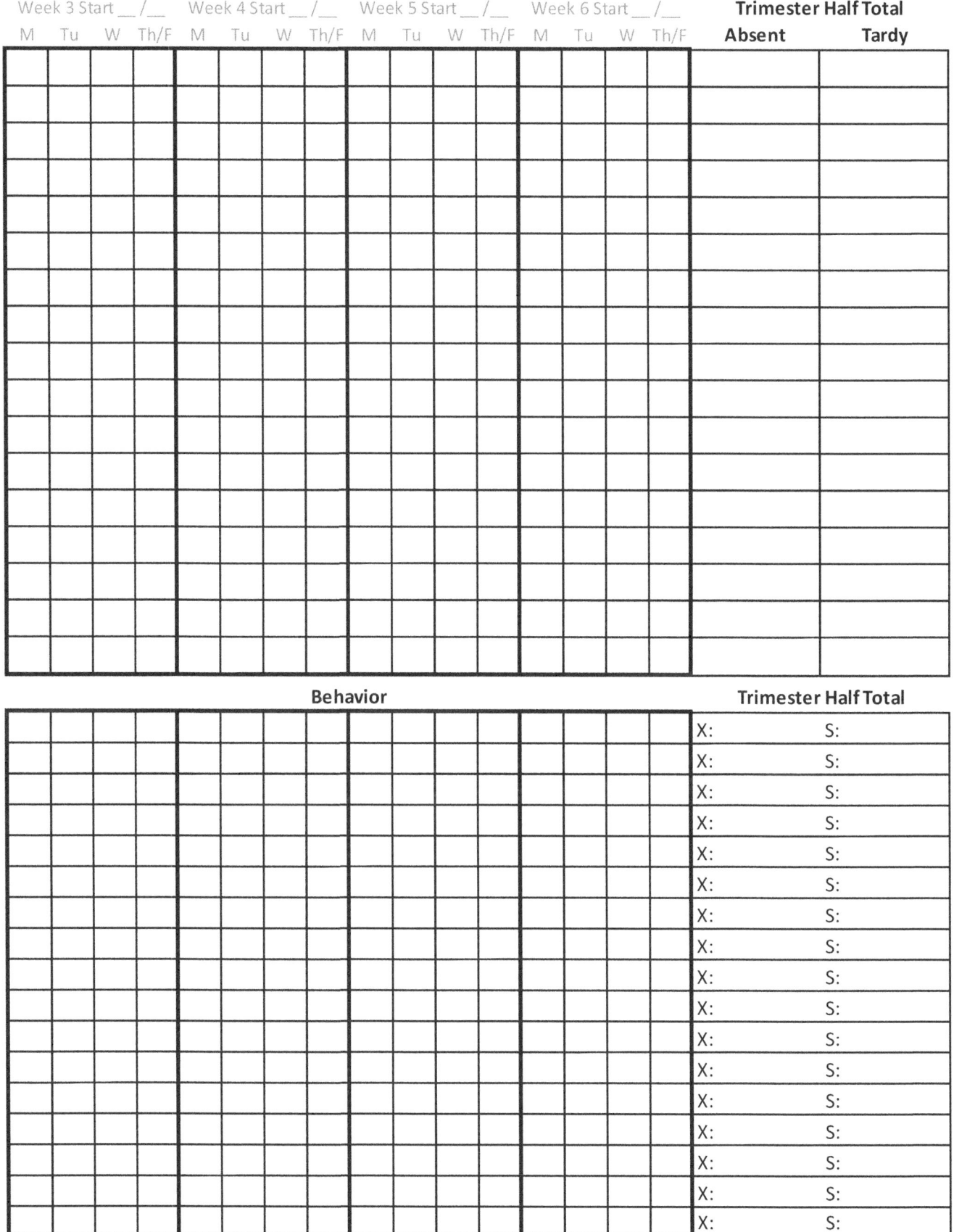

Trimester 1

Attendance and Behavior

Student Full Name Please spell names correctly.	Parent Name	Reg (✓)	Phone Number	Attendance								
				Week 7 Start __/__				Week 8 Start __/__			
				M	Tu	W	Th/F	M	Tu	W	Th/F
1											
2											
3											
4											
5											
6											
7											
8											
9											
10											
11											
12											
13											
14											
15											
16											
17											

Key

Attendance

- ✓ Present
- A Absent
- T Tardy
- S Sick
- L Confirmed as Last Day (Cancel)

Behavior

X Behavioral Violation
- Not following teacher's directions and class rules
- Making fun of or being rude to fellow students
- Misbehaving during prayer
- Excessive roughness during play
- Wearing clothes to school that are unclean

S Severe Behavioral Violation
- Fighting with, beating, physically harming others
- Using vulgar language
- Intentionally damaging/stealing others' property
- Insubordination, rude behavior to teacher; Cheating
- Taunting based on race, color, language
- Lewd and inappropriate dressing

Behavior

#								
1								
2								
3								
4								
5								
6								
7								
8								
9								
10								
11								
12								
13								
14								
15								
16								
17								

Trimester 1

Attendance and Behavior

Attendance

Week 9 Start __/__				Week 10 Start __/__				Week 11 Start __/__				Week 12 Start __/__				Trimester Total	
M	Tu	W	Th/F	M	Tu	W	Th/F	M	Tu	W	Th/F	M	Tu	W	Th/F	Absent	Tardy

Behavior

																Trimester Total	
																X:	S:
																X:	S:
																X:	S:
																X:	S:
																X:	S:
																X:	S:
																X:	S:
																X:	S:
																X:	S:
																X:	S:
																X:	S:
																X:	S:
																X:	S:
																X:	S:
																X:	S:
																X:	S:
																X:	S:

Trimester 1

Attendance and Behavior

Student Full Name (Please spell names correctly.)	Parent Name	Reg (✓)	Phone Number	Attendance Week 1 Start __/__				Week 2 Start __/__			
				M	Tu	W	Th/F	M	Tu	W	Th/F
1											
2											
3											
4											
5											
6											
7											
8											
9											
10											
11											
12											
13											
14											
15											
16											
17											

Key

Attendance
- ✓ Present
- **A** Absent
- **T** Tardy
- **S** Sick
- **L** Confirmed as Last Day (Cancel)

Behavior
- **X** Behavioral Violation
    - Not following teacher's directions and class rules
    - Making fun of or being rude to fellow students
    - Misbehaving during prayer
    - Excessive roughness during play
    - Wearing clothes to school that are unclean
- **S** Severe Behavioral Violation
    - Fighting with, beating, physically harming others
    - Using vulgar language
    - Intentionally damaging/stealing others' property
    - Insubordination, rude behavior to teacher; Cheating
    - Taunting based on race, color, language
    - Lewd and inappropriate dressing

Behavior

#								
1								
2								
3								
4								
5								
6								
7								
8								
9								
10								
11								
12								
13								
14								
15								
16								
17								

Trimester 2

Attendance and Behavior

Attendance

Week 3 Start __/__				Week 4 Start __/__				Week 5 Start __/__				Week 6 Start __/__				Trimester Half Total	
M	Tu	W	Th/F	M	Tu	W	Th/F	M	Tu	W	Th/F	M	Tu	W	Th/F	Absent	Tardy

Behavior

																Trimester Half Total	
																X:	S:
																X:	S:
																X:	S:
																X:	S:
																X:	S:
																X:	S:
																X:	S:
																X:	S:
																X:	S:
																X:	S:
																X:	S:
																X:	S:
																X:	S:
																X:	S:
																X:	S:
																X:	S:
																X:	S:

Trimester 2

Attendance and Behavior

Student Full Name Please spell names correctly.	Parent Name	Reg (✓)	Phone Number	Attendance								
				Week 7 Start __/__				Week 8 Start __/__			
				M	Tu	W	Th/F	M	Tu	W	Th/F
1											
2											
3											
4											
5											
6											
7											
8											
9											
10											
11											
12											
13											
14											
15											
16											
17											

Key

Attendance
- ✓ Present
- **A** Absent
- **T** Tardy
- **S** Sick
- **L** Confirmed as Last Day (Cancel)

Behavior
- **X** Behavioral Violation
    - Not following teacher's directions and class rules
    - Making fun of or being rude to fellow students
    - Misbehaving during prayer
    - Excessive roughness during play
    - Wearing clothes to school that are unclean
- **S** Severe Behavioral Violation
    - Fighting with, beating, physically harming others
    - Using vulgar language
    - Intentionally damaging/stealing others' property
    - Insubordination, rude behavior to teacher; Cheating
    - Taunting based on race, color, language
    - Lewd and inappropriate dressing

Behavior

#								
1								
2								
3								
4								
5								
6								
7								
8								
9								
10								
11								
12								
13								
14								
15								
16								
17								

Trimester 2

Attendance and Behavior

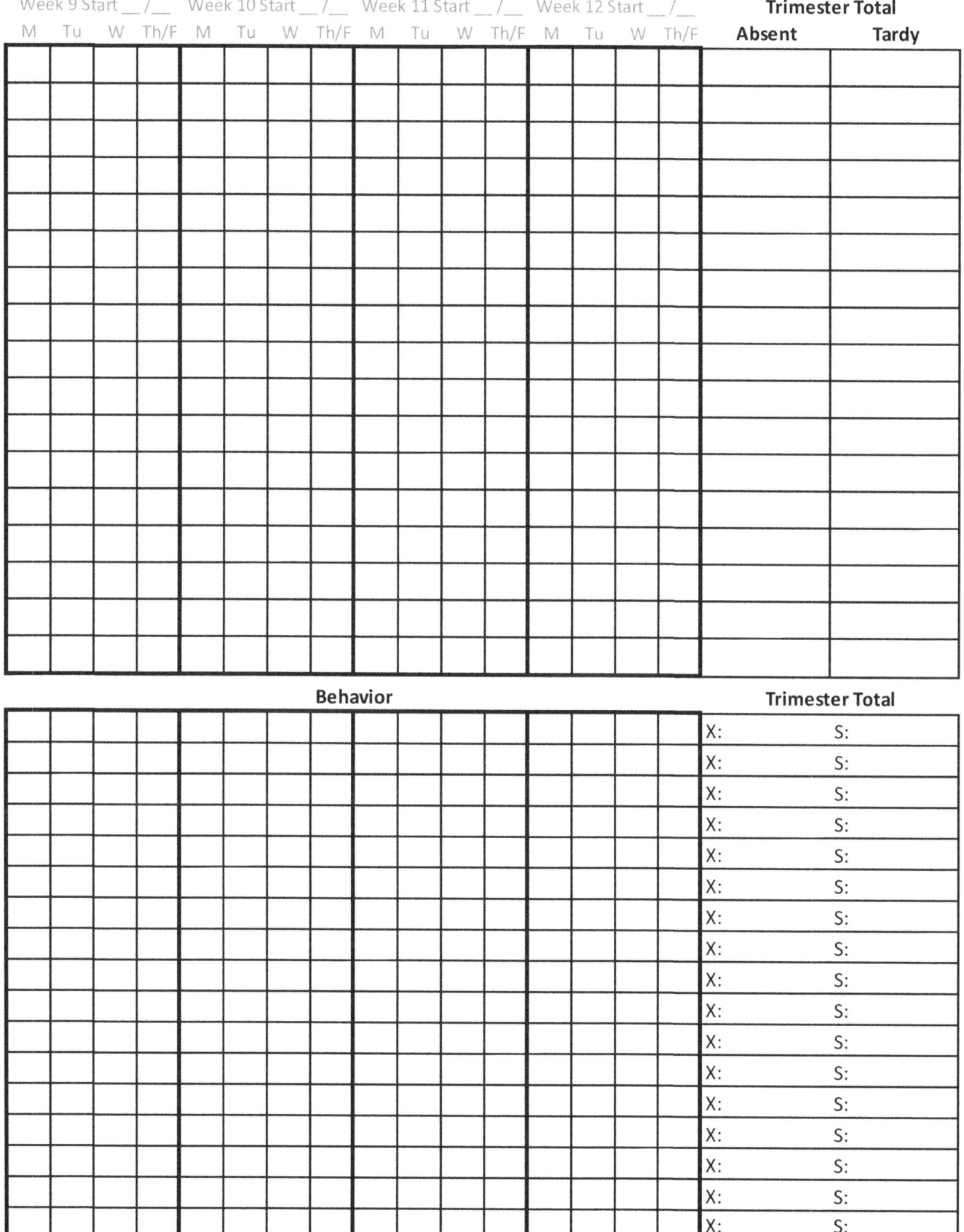

Trimester 2

Attendance and Behavior

Student Full Name Please spell names correctly.	Parent Name	Reg (✓)	Phone Number	Attendance							
				Week 1 Start __/__				Week 2 Start __/__			
				M	Tu	W	Th/F	M	Tu	W	Th/F
1											
2											
3											
4											
5											
6											
7											
8											
9											
10											
11											
12											
13											
14											
15											
16											
17											

Key

Attendance
- ✓ Present
- **A** Absent
- **T** Tardy
- **S** Sick
- **L** Confirmed as Last Day (Cancel)

Behavior
- **X** Behavioral Violation
    - Not following teacher's directions and class rules
    - Making fun of or being rude to fellow students
    - Misbehaving during prayer
    - Excessive roughness during play
    - Wearing clothes to school that are unclean
- **S** Severe Behavioral Violation
    - Fighting with, beating, physically harming others
    - Using vulgar language
    - Intentionally damaging/stealing others' property
    - Insubordination, rude behavior to teacher; Cheating
    - Taunting based on race, color, language
    - Lewd and inappropriate dressing

Behavior

#							
1							
2							
3							
4							
5							
6							
7							
8							
9							
10							
11							
12							
13							
14							
15							
16							
17							

Trimester 3

Attendance and Behavior

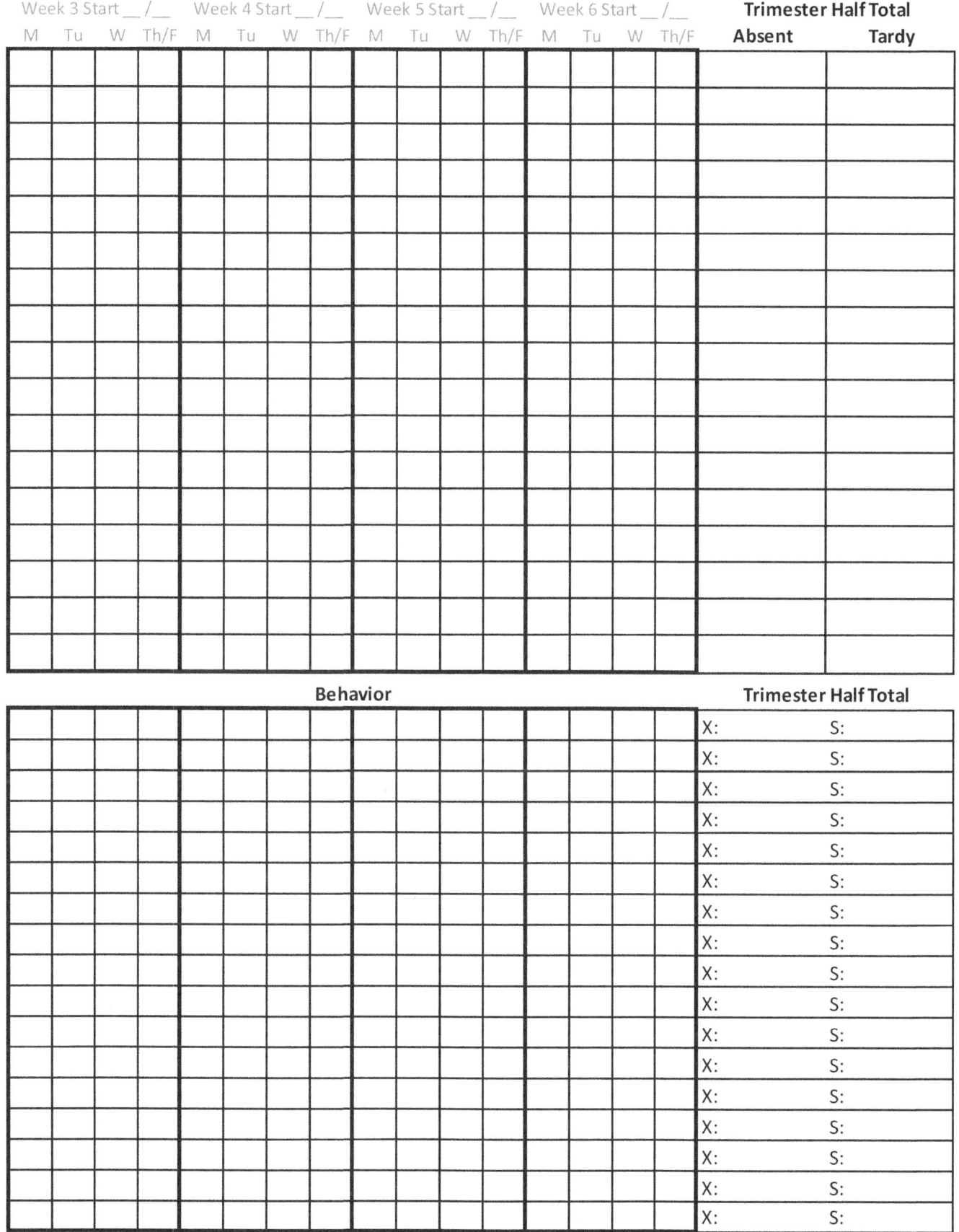

Trimester 3

Attendance and Behavior

Student Full Name Please spell names correctly.	Parent Name	Reg (✓)	Phone Number	Attendance Week 7 Start __/__				Week 8 Start __/__			
				M	Tu	W	Th/F	M	Tu	W	Th/F
1											
2											
3											
4											
5											
6											
7											
8											
9											
10											
11											
12											
13											
14											
15											
16											
17											

Key

Attendance
- ✓ Present
- **A** Absent
- **T** Tardy
- **S** Sick
- **L** Confirmed as Last Day (Cancel)

Behavior
- **X** Behavioral Violation
  - Not following teacher's directions and class rules
  - Making fun of or being rude to fellow students
  - Misbehaving during prayer
  - Excessive roughness during play
  - Wearing clothes to school that are unclean
- **S** Severe Behavioral Violation
  - Fighting with, beating, physically harming others
  - Using vulgar language
  - Intentionally damaging/stealing others' property
  - Insubordination, rude behavior to teacher; Cheating
  - Taunting based on race, color, language
  - Lewd and inappropriate dressing

Behavior

#	M	Tu	W	Th/F	M	Tu	W	Th/F
1								
2								
3								
4								
5								
6								
7								
8								
9								
10								
11								
12								
13								
14								
15								
16								
17								

Trimester 3

Attendance and Behavior

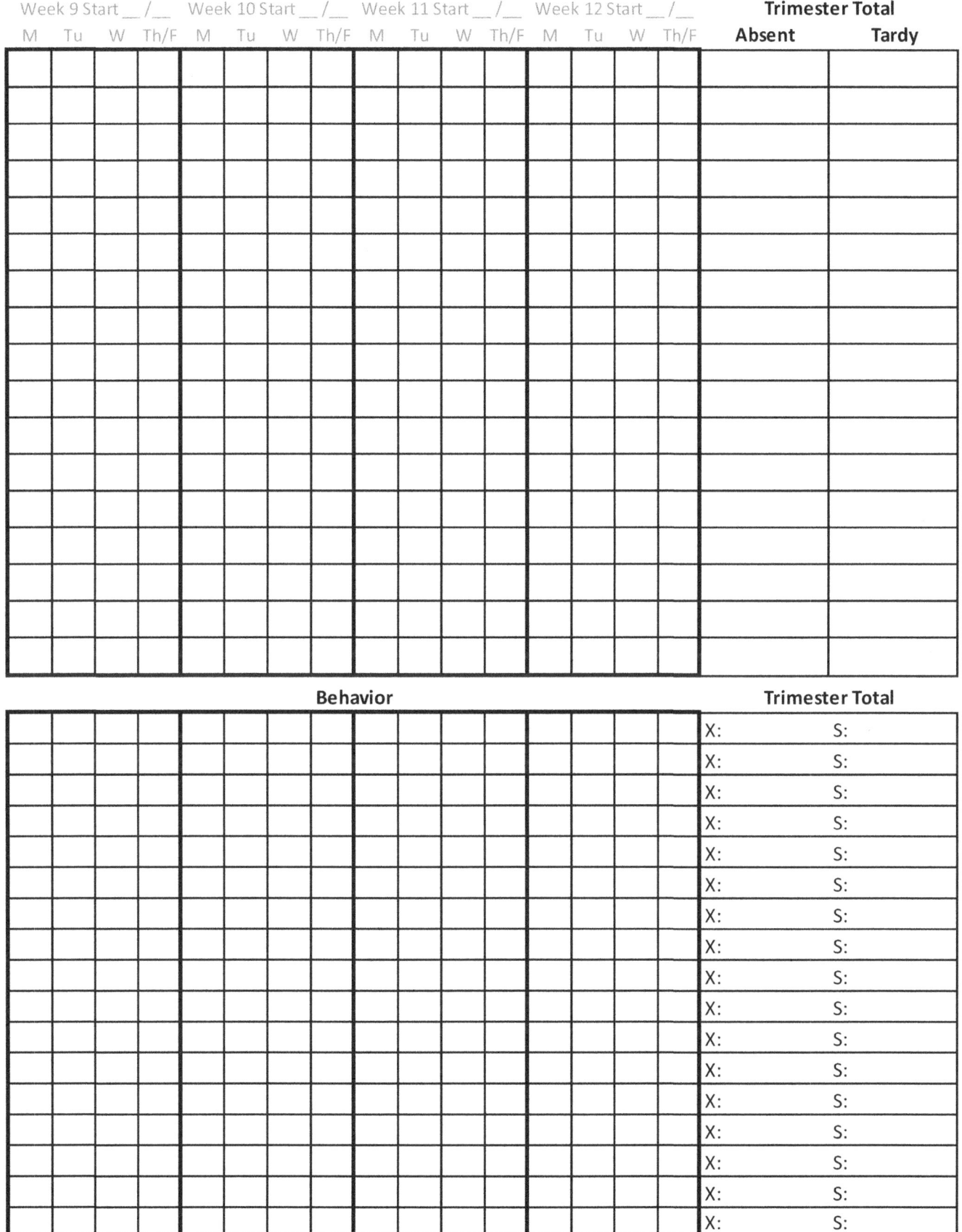

Trimester 3

Quran Reading Rubric

Fluency (# Lines of 15 Line Quran in 3 Min / # Mistakes Incuding Makharij but Not Tajwid Rules)

Trimester 1

Student Name	Week															
	1	2	3	4	5	6	7	8	9	10	11	12	1	2	3	4

Makharij and Harakat (Letter Articulation and Vowels) (Check when each is correct.)

	Weeks 1-6	Weeks 7-12	Weeks 1-6
Student Name	ذ ق ص ض ط ظ ع غ حركات ث ح	ذ ق ص ض ط ظ ع غ حركات ث ح	ذ ق ص ض ط ظ ع غ حركات ث ح

Quran Reading Rubric

Fluency (# Lines of 15 Line Quran in 3 Min / # Mistakes Including Makharij but Not Tajwid Rules)

Trimester 2 Week								Trimester 3 Week									
5	6	7	8	9	10	11	12	1	2	3	4	5	6	7	8	9	10	11	12

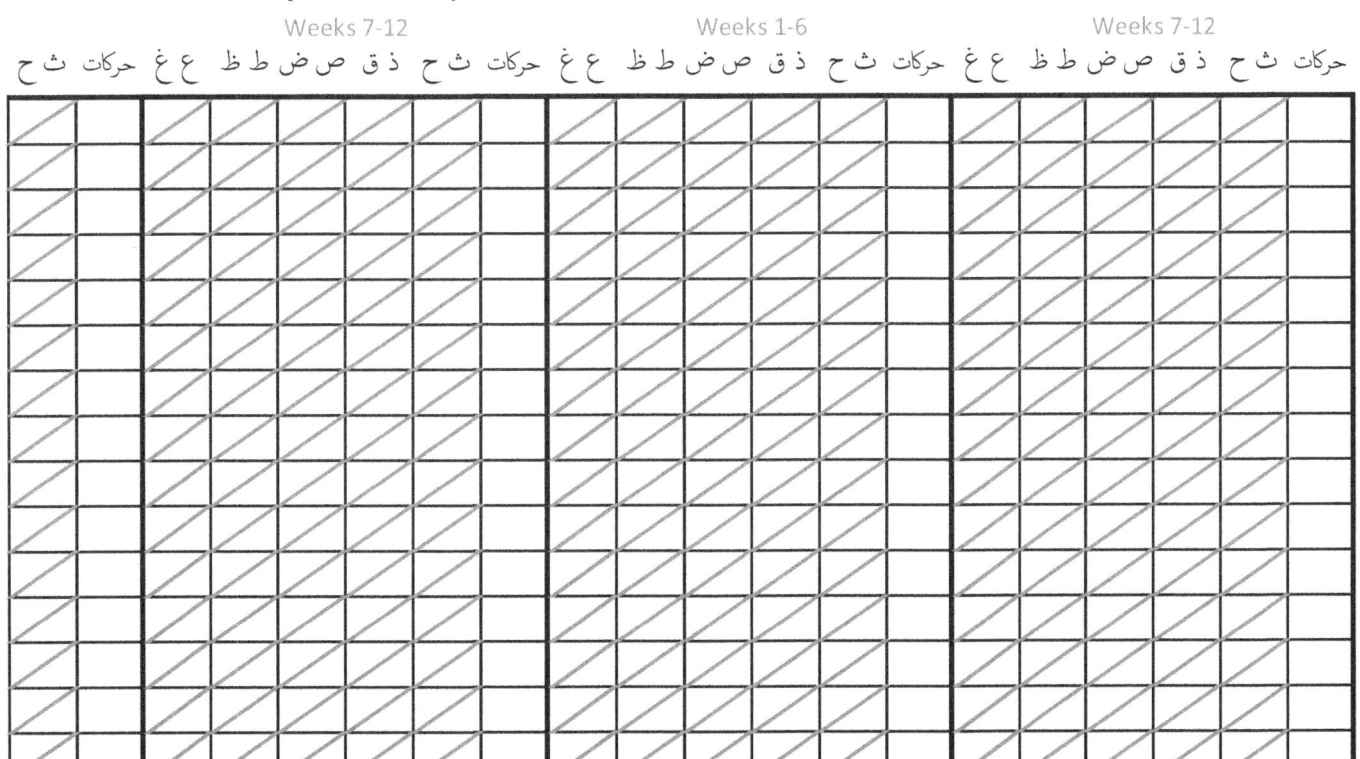

Makharij and Harakat (Letter Articulation and Vowels) (Check when each is correct.)

Weeks 7-12	Weeks 1-6	Weeks 7-12
حركات ث ح ذ ق ص ض ط ظ ع غ	حركات ث ح ذ ق ص ض ط ظ ع غ	حركات ث ح ذ ق ص ض ط ظ ع غ

Comprehensive Assessment (Elementary Grades)

Grade: _____ Year: 20___ - 20___

Student: _____

Subject	Grade Qaidah Skill	Score	Grade 1 Skill	Score	Grade 2 Skill	Score	Grade 3 Skill	Score
Quran Reading and Tajwid	Pronunciation (alphabet) (Q1)		Ta'wudh, Mim Nun Mushadadah (T14,15)		Ta'wudh, Mim Nun Mushadadah (T14,15)		Reading Fluency: 11 Quran lines, 3 min	
	Letter Recognition (mixed, joined) (Q2)		Qalqalah (T16), Lam of Allah (T17a)		Qalqalah (T16), Lam of Allah (T17a)		Revise, Identify Tajwid Rules T14-T17a	
	Fluency Word, Adv Letter Recog (Q3,4)		Reading Fluency: 5 Quran lines, 3 min		Reading Fluency: 9 Quran lines, 3 min		Reading Fluency: 13 Quran lines, 3 min	
	Harakah (fatha, kasra, dama, tanwin) (Q5)		Ra Mutaharrikah, Sakinah (T17b,c)		Ra Mutaharrikah, Sakinah (T17b,c)		Revise, Identify Tajwid Rules T17b-T18c	
	Stretched Harakahs (stretch, lin) (Q6)		Full-Mouth Letters, Alif (T17d,e)		Full-Mouth Letters, Alif (T17d,e)		Reading Fluency: 15 Quran lines, 3 min	
	Joining Letters (sukun, shad), Madd (Q7,8)		Ikhfa, Idgham, Izhar Shafwi (T18a,b,c)		Ikhfa, Idgham, Izhar Shafwi (T18a,b,c)		Revise, Identify Tajwid Rules T19a-T20e	
	Special Cases, Fluency in 3 Words (Q9,10)		Qalb, Idgham wo/w Ghunnah (T19a,b,c)		Qalb, Idgham wo/w Ghunnah (T19a,b,c)			
	Stopping, Fluency in One Line (Q11,12,13)		Izhar, Ikhfa (T19d,e), Madd (T20a,b,c,d,e)		Izhar, Ikhfa (T19d,e), Madd (T20a,b,c,d,e)			
	All Makharij are Correct		Reading Fluency: 7 Quran lines, 3 min		Reading Fluency: 11 Quran lines, 3 min			
Quran Memorization	Surah Fatihah		Surah Fil		Surah 'Adiyat		Surah Inshirah*	
	Surah Ikhlas		Surah Quraish		Surah Qari'ah		Surah Tin*	
	Surah Falaq		Surah Ma'un		Surah Takathur		Surah Alaq*	
	Surah Nas		Surah Kawthar, Kafirun		Surah Asr		Surah Qadr*	
			Surah Nasr		Surah Humazah		Surah Bayyinah*	
			Surah Lahab				Surah Zilzal*	
Kalimah and Dua Memorization	First Kalimah with Meaning		Takbir Tahrima		Tashahhud		Qunut	
	Second Kalimah with Meaning		Dua Al-Istifta (Thana)				Dua to Make for Parent	
	Ta'awudh, Time Eating, Time Sleeping							
	Greeting Muslim, Reply to Salam		Tasbih of Ruku		Durud Ibrahim		Entering a House*	
	Drink Water, Hear Messenger (S) Name		Rising from Ruku		After Durud Ibrahim		Leaving a House*	
	We Sneeze, Other Sneezes, Reply Snzng*		In Qawmah		Before Wudu*		When Breaking the Fast	
	Entering Washroom, Leaving Washroom*		Tasbih of Sajdah		After Wudu		When Traveling	
	After Eating, Forget to Recite at Eating		Between Two Sajdah*		Entering the Masjid		Dua to Make for Host*	
	Waking Up		Completing the Salah		Leaving the Masjid*			
Islamic Studies			Intro 5 Pillars, Intro Taharah, Wudu Method (N1)		Cleaning Methods, Wudu Detail, Tayam, Salah Method (N2)		Najas Typ, Ghusl, SalaRakt/Cond/Naw, Witr, Musaf, Mard (N3)	
			Feed Hungry, Help, Calmness, Purity, Truth (N1)*		Truth, Salam, Right Hand, Drink, Neighbors (N2)*		Salah, Love Steadfst, Life, Dua, Guest, Mercy, Shukr (N3)*	
			Childhood, Youth, Marriage Khadijah, Children (N1)		Hira Revelation, 1st Believers, Open Cal, Persecut (N2)		Abyssinia, Boycott, Year Sorrow, Taif, Invitation, Miraj (N3)	
			Adam (a), Nuh (a) (N1)		Hud (a), Salih (a) (N2)		Ibrahim (a), Ismail (a), Ishaq (a) (N3)	
			7 Articles, Who is Allah, Provider, Merciful (N1)		Protector, Hearer, Seer, One; Angel; Book; Quran (N2)		Messengers, Qiyamah, Minor Signs, Major Signs (N3)	
			Respect, Cleanliness, Polite, Smile, Right Side (N1)*		Promises, Thanking, Salam, Helping, Animals (N2)*		Thinking Good, Sharing, Parents, Truth, Good Word (N3)*	
			Eat, Drink, Sleeping, Waking, Washroom (N1)*		Greeting, Enter House, Speak, Sneeze, Yawn (N2)*		Traveling, Studying, Quran, Walking, Masjid (N3)*	

Adab Akhlaqaid Tark StarHadi Fiqh

Scoring Key: ✓ Skill acquired prior to this year + Skill acquired this academic year <Blank> Skill not yet acquired or not tested / * Not required for students revising prior grades / **Q** Safar Qaidah Level, **T** Safar Tajwid Level, **N** Nasihah Grade

Examiner Name & Date	
Comments	

Teachers: Complete and mark all scores and comments up to and including current grade, in pen. **Examiners:** Complete and mark only on top of scores marked by teachers, in thick pen. Add comments in pen.

Copyright © 2019 by Masjid Uthman (Uthman Academy, Uthman Seminary)

Comprehensive Assessment (Middle Grades)

Student: _____ Grade: _____ Year: 20___ - 20___

Subject	Skill (Grade 4)	Score	Skill (Grade 5)	Score	Skill (Grade 6)	Score	Skill (Grade 7)	Score
Quran Reading and Tajwid	Reading Fluency: 15 Quran lines, 3 min		Reading Fluency: 15 Quran lines, 2 min					
	Revise, Identify Tajwid Rules T14-T17a		Revise, Identify Tajwid Rules T14-T17a					
	Reading Fluency: 15 Quran lines, 2.5 min		Reading Fluency: 15 Quran lines, 2 min					
	Revise, Identify Tajwid Rules T17b-T18c		Revise, Identify Tajwid Rules T17b-T18c					
	Reading Fluency: 15 Quran lines, 2 min		Reading Fluency: 15 Quran lines, 2 min					
	Revise, Identify Tajwid Rules T19a-T20e		Revise, Identify Tajwid Rules T19a-T20e					
Quran Memorization	Surah Fajr*		Surah Yasin Ruku 1*		Surah Yasin Ruku 3*			
	Surah Balad*							
	Surah Shams*							
	Surah Layl*		Surah Yasin Ruku 2*		Surah Yasin Ruku 4*			
	Surah Dhuha*							
	Ayat Al-Kursi				Surah Yasin Ruku 5*			
Kalimah and Dua Memorization	Adhan		Protection from Calamities*		Returning from Journey*		Most Comprehensive Dua*	
	Extra Words for Fajr Adhan		At Conclusion of a Gathering				Talbiyah*	
	Reply to Words of Adhan*		When Visiting the Sick*		Protection from Evil Eye		Takbir of Tashriq*	
	After Adhan*		When in Distress*		Sayyidul Istighfar		When Visiting Graveyard	
			When Feeling Anger*				Time of Burying Deceased*	
	Janazah Dua		Dua at Time of Need (Hajah)		When in Market Place*		To Benefit from Knowledge*	
	Janazah Dua Male Infant*		Dua on Laylatul Qadr*		When Having Nightmare		At the Time of Death*	
	Janazah Dua Female Infant*							
Islamic Studies (Adab Akhlaq, Aqaid, Tarikh, Sirah, Hadi, Fiqh)	Khuff,Masah Wound,Salah Wajib,Sahw,Sawm,Taraw(N4)		Tayam,Salah Sunan,Salah Time,Masbuq,Qada,Id,Hajj(N5)		Water,Impur,Matur,Imam,Salah Wajib,Janaiz,Jumah(N6)		Salah Makr,Saj,Tilawa,Qasr,Zaka,Inherit,Itikaf,Food(N7)	
	Feeding,Racism,Thank,Friend,Trust,Paradise,Zikr(N4)		Promises,Tongue,Ghibah,Intox,99Names,Charact(N5)*		Major Sins,Pride,Health,Truth,Love Messeng,Parent(N6)*		People of Jann/Jahan,Ghibah,Modest,Salah Jamah(N7)*	
	Aqaba,Hijra,Treaties,Hypocrit,Badr,Uhud,Ahzab(N4)		Hudaibia,Conquest Makkah,Hunain,Tabuk,Farewell(N5)		Shamail,Abu Bakr(r),Life & Work, Mother Believers(N6)		Shamail,Umar(r),Life and Work(N7)	
	Yaqub(a),Yusuf(a)(N4)		Musa(a),Isa(a)(N5)		Dawud(a),Sulayman(a),Yunus(a),Umayyads(N6)		Zakariyyah(a),Yahya,(a),Abbasids(N7)	
	Mahdi/Dajjal/Yajuj/Beast,Trumpet,Qiyama,Bridge(N4)		Death,Janna,Jahanam,Taqdir,Allah/Prophet/Sahaba(N5)		Ahl Sunnah,Prophet,Khulafa,Ash Mubash,Mujiza(N6)		Qada and Qadr,Evil Eye,Life after Death,Barzakh(N7)	
	Trust,Permission Enter,Remov Harm,Neighbor(N4)*		Mashwara,Patience,Kinship,Gifts,Guest,Dhikr(N5)*		Oppression,Bullying,Envy,Ghibah,Pride,Sunnah(N6)*		Spreading Rumors,Value of Time,Knowledge,Durud(N7)*	
	Dua,Dress,Guest/Host,Gathering,Istinja(N4)*		Ghusl,Social Interaction,Writing,Swak,Visit Sick(N5)*		Adhan,Modest Dress,Moderation Expend,Hygiene(N6)*		5 Branches,Faith,Oaths,Phone,Elders,Non-Muslims(N7)*	

Scoring Key: ✓ Skill acquired prior to this year + Skill acquired this academic year <Blank> Skill not yet acquired or not tested / * Not required for students revising prior grades / **Q** Safar Qaidah Level, **T** Safar Tajwid Level, **N** Nasihah Grade

Examiner				
Name & Date				
Most Recent Comments				

Copyright © 2019 by Masjid Uthman (Uthman Academy, Uthman Seminary)

Teachers: Complete and mark all scores and comments up to and including current grade, in pen. **Examiners:** Complete and mark only on top of scores marked by teachers, in thick pen. Add comments in pen.

Comprehensive Assessment (Elementary Grades)

Student: _____ Grade: _____ Year: 20___ - 20___

Subject		Grade Qaidah		Grade 1		Grade 2		Grade 3	
		Skill	Score	Skill	Score	Skill	Score	Skill	Score
Quran Reading and Tajwid		Pronunciation (alphabet) (Q1)		Ta'wudh, Mim Nun Mushadadah (T14,15)		Ta'wudh, Mim Nun Mushadadah (T14,15)		Reading Fluency: 11 Quran lines, 3 min	
		Letter Recognition (mixed, joined) (Q2)		Qalqalah (T16), Lam of Allah (T17a)		Qalqalah (T16), Lam of Allah (T17a)		Revise, Identify Tajwid Rules T14-T17a	
		Fluency Word, Adv Letter Recog (Q3,4)		Reading Fluency: 5 Quran lines, 3 min		Reading Fluency: 9 Quran lines, 3 min		Reading Fluency: 13 Quran lines, 3 min	
		Harakah (fatha, kasra, dama, tanwin) (Q5)		Ra Mutaharrikah, Sakinah (T17b,c)		Ra Mutaharrikah, Sakinah (T17b,c)		Revise, Identify Tajwid Rules T17b-T18c	
		Stretched Harakahs (stretch, lin) (Q6)		Full-Mouth Letters, Alif (T17d,e)		Full-Mouth Letters, Alif (T17d,e)		Reading Fluency: 15 Quran lines, 3 min	
		Joining Letters (sukun, shad), Madd (Q7,8)		Ikhfa, Idgham, Izhar Shafwi (T18a,b,c)		Ikhfa, Idgham, Izhar Shafwi (T18a,b,c)		Revise, Identify Tajwid Rules T19a-T20e	
		Special Cases, Fluency in 3 Words (Q9,10)		Qalb, Idgham wo/w Ghunnah (T19a,b,c)		Qalb, Idgham wo/w Ghunnah (T19a,b,c)			
		Stopping, Fluency in One Line (Q11,12,13)		Izhar, Ikhfa (T19d,e), Madd (T20a,b,c,d,e)		Izhar, Ikhfa (T19d,e), Madd (T20a,b,c,d,e)			
		All Makharij are Correct		Reading Fluency: 7 Quran lines, 3 min		Reading Fluency: 11 Quran lines, 3 min			
Quran Memorization		Surah Fatihah		Surah Fil		Surah 'Adiyat		Surah Inshirah*	
		Surah Ikhlas		Surah Quraish		Surah Qari'ah		Surah Tin*	
		Surah Falaq		Surah Ma'un		Surah Takathur		Surah Alaq*	
		Surah Nas		Surah Kawthar, Kafirun		Surah Asr		Surah Qadr*	
				Surah Nasr		Surah Humazah		Surah Bayyinah*	
				Surah Lahab				Surah Zilzal*	
Kalimah and Dua Memorization		First Kalimah with Meaning		Takbir Tahrima		Tashahhud		Qunut	
		Second Kalimah with Meaning		Dua Al-Istifta (Thana)				Dua to Make for Parent	
		Ta'awudh, Time Eating, Time Sleeping							
		Greeting Muslim, Reply to Salam		Tasbih of Ruku		Durud Ibrahim		Entering a House*	
		Drink Water, Hear Messenger (S) Name		Rising from Ruku		After Durud Ibrahim		Leaving a House*	
		We Sneeze, Other Sneezes, Reply Snzng*		In Qawmah		Before Wudu*		When Breaking the Fast	
		Entering Washroom, Leaving Washroom*		Tasbih of Sajdah		After Wudu		When Traveling	
		After Eating, Forget to Recite at Eating		Between Two Sajdah*		Entering the Masjid		Dua to Make for Host*	
		Waking Up		Completing the Salah		Leaving the Masjid*			
Islamic Studies	Adab Akhlaq Aqaid Tarikh Hadi Sira Fiqh			Intro 5 Pillars, Intro Taharah, Wudu Method (N1)		Cleaning Methods, Wudu Detail, Tayam, Salah Method (N2)		Najas Typ, Ghusl, SalahRakt/Cond/Naw, Witr, Musaf, Mard (N3)	
				Feed Hungry, Help, Calmness, Purity, Truth (N1)*		Truth, Salam, Right Hand, Drink, Neighbors (N2)*		Salah, Love, Steadfst, Life, Dua, Guest, Mercy, Shukr (N3)*	
				Childhood, Youth, Marriage Khadijah, Children (N1)		Hira, Revelation, 1st Believers, Open Call, Persecut (N2)		Abyssinia, Boycott, Year Sorrow, Taif, Invitation, Miraj (N3)	
				Adam (a), Nuh (a) (N1)		Hud (a), Salih (a) (N2)		Ibrahim (a), Ismail (a), Ishaq (a) (N3)	
				7 Articles, Who is Allah, Provider, Merciful (N1)		Protector, Hearer, Seer, One; Angel; Book; Quran (N2)		Messengers, Qiyamah, Minor Signs, Major Signs (N3)	
				Respect, Cleanliness, Polite, Smile, Right Side (N1)*		Promises, Thanking, Salam, Helping, Animals (N2)*		Thinking Good, Sharing, Parents, Truth, Good Word (N3)*	
				Eat, Drink, Sleeping, Waking, Washroom (N1)*		Greeting, Enter House, Speak, Sneeze, Yawn (N2)*		Traveling, Studying, Quran, Walking, Masjid (N3)*	

Scoring Key: ✓ Skill acquired prior to this year / + Skill acquired this academic year / <Blank> Skill not yet acquired or not tested / * Not required for students revising prior grades / **Q** Safar Qaidah Level, **T** Safar Tajwid Level, **N** Nasihah Grade

Examiner Name & Date: _____

Comments: _____

Copyright © 2019 by Masjid Uthman (Uthman Academy, Uthman Seminary)

Teachers: Complete and mark all scores and comments up to and including current grade, in pen. Examiners: Complete and mark only on top of scores marked by teachers, in thick pen. Add comments in pen.

Comprehensive Assessment (Middle Grades)

Subject | Student: _____ Grade: _____ Year: 20___ - 20___

Subject		Grade 4		Grade 5		Grade 6		Grade 7	
		Skill	Score	Skill	Score	Skill	Score	Skill	Score
Quran Reading and Tajwid		Reading Fluency: 15 Quran lines, 3 min		Reading Fluency: 15 Quran lines, 2 min					
		Revise, Identify Tajwid Rules T14-T17a		Revise, Identify Tajwid Rules T14-T17a					
		Reading Fluency: 15 Quran lines, 2.5 min		Reading Fluency: 15 Quran lines, 2 min					
		Revise, Identify Tajwid Rules T17b-T18c		Revise, Identify Tajwid Rules T17b-T18c					
		Reading Fluency: 15 Quran lines, 2 min		Reading Fluency: 15 Quran lines, 2 min					
		Revise, Identify Tajwid Rules T19a-T20e		Revise, Identify Tajwid Rules T19a-T20e					
Quran Memorization		Surah Fajr*		Surah Yasin Ruku 1*		Surah Yasin Ruku 3*			
		Surah Balad*							
		Surah Shams*		Surah Yasin Ruku 2*		Surah Yasin Ruku 4*			
		Surah Layl*							
		Surah Dhuha*				Surah Yasin Ruku 5*			
		Ayat Al-Kursi							
Kalimah and Dua Memorization		Adhan		Protection from Calamities*				Most Comprehensive Dua*	
		Extra Words for Fajr Adhan		At Conclusion of a Gathering		Returning from Journey*		Talbiyah*	
		Reply to Words of Adhan*		When Visiting the Sick*		Protection from Evil Eye		Takbir of Tashriq*	
		After Adhan*		When in Distress*		Sayyidul Istighfar		When Visiting Graveyard	
		Janazah Dua		When Feeling Anger*		When in Market Place*		Time of Burying Deceased*	
		Janazah Dua Male Infant*		Dua at Time of Need (Hajah)		When Having Nightmare		To Benefit from Knowledge*	
		Janazah Dua Female Infant*		Dua on Laylatul Qadr*				At the Time of Death*	
Islamic Studies	Adab	Khuff,Masah Wound,Salah Wajib,Sahw,Sawm,Taraw(N4)		Tayam,Salah Sunan,Salah Time,Masbuq,Qada,Id Hajj(N5)		Water,Impur,Matur,Imam,Salah Wajib,Janaiz,Jumah (N6)		Salah Makr,Saj,Tilawa,Qas r,Zaka,Inherit,Itikaf,Food(N7)	
	Akhlaq	Feeding,Racism,Thank,Friend,Trust,Paradise,Zikr(N4)*		Promises,Tongue,Ghibah,Intox,99Names,Charac t (N5)*		Major Sins,Pride,Health,Truth,Love Messeng,Parent (N6)*		PeopledJann/Jahan, Ghibah, Modest,Salah Jamah (N7)*	
	Aqaid	Aqaba,Hijra,Treaties,Hypocrit,Badr,Uhud,Ahzab(N4)		Hudaibia,Conquest Makkah,Hunan,Tabuk,Farewell (N5)		Shamail,Abu Bakr (r), Life & Work, Mother Believers (N6)		Shamail, Umar (r), Life and Work (N7)	
	Tark Hadi	Yaqub (a), Yusuf (a) (N4)		Musa (a), Isa (a) (N5)		Dawud (a), Sulayman (a), Yunus (a), Umayyads (N6)		Zakariyyah (a), Yahya, (a), Abbasids (N7)	
	Sirah	Mahdy/Dajjal/Yajuj/Beast,Trumpet,Qiyama,Bridge(N4)		Death,Janna,Jahanam,Taqdir, Allah/Prophet/Sahaba (N5)		Ahl Sunnah,Prophet,Khulafa,Ash Mubash,Mujiza (N6)		Qada and Qadr, Evil Eye, Life after Death, Barzakh (N7)	
	Fiqh	Trust, Permission Enter, Remov Harm, Neighbor (N4)*		Mashwara, Patience, Kinship, Gifts, Guest, Dhikr (N5)*		Oppression, Bullying, Envy, Ghibah, Pride, Sunnah (N6)*		Spreading Rumors, Value of Time, Knowledge, Durud (N7)*	
		Dua, Dress, Guest/Host, Gathering, Istinja (N4)*		Ghusl, Social Interaction, Writing, Siwak, Visit Sick (N5)*		Adhan, Modest Dress, Moderation Expend, Hygiene (N6)*		5 Branches Faith, Oaths,Phone, Elders, Non-Muslims (N7)*	

Scoring Key: ✓ Skill acquired prior to this year + Skill acquired this academic year <Blank> Skill not yet acquired or not tested / * Not required for students revising prior grades / **Q** Safar Qaidah Level, **T** Safar Tajwid Level, **N** Nasihah Grade

Examiner	
Name & Date	
Most Recent Comments	

Copyright © 2019 by Masjid Uthman (Uthman Academy, Uthman Seminary)

Teachers: Complete and mark all scores and comments up to and including current grade, in pen. **Examiners:** Complete and mark only on top of scores marked by teachers, in thick pen. Add comments in pen.

Comprehensive Assessment (Elementary Grades)

Student: _____ Grade: _____ Year: 20____ - 20____

Subject		Grade Qaidah		Grade 1		Grade 2		Grade 3	
		Skill	Score	Skill	Score	Skill	Score	Skill	Score
Quran Reading and Tajwid		Pronunciation (alphabet) (Q1)		Ta'wudh, Mim Nun Mushadadah (T14,15)		Ta'wudh, Mim Nun Mushadadah (T14,15)		Reading Fluency: 11 Quran lines, 3 min	
		Letter Recognition (mixed, joined) (Q2)		Qalqalah (T16), Lam of Allah (T17a)		Qalqalah (T16), Lam of Allah (T17a)		Revise, Identify Tajwid Rules T14-T17a	
		Fluency Word, Adv Letter Recog (Q3,4)		Reading Fluency: 5 Quran lines, 3 min		Reading Fluency: 9 Quran lines, 3 min		Reading Fluency: 13 Quran lines, 3 min	
		Harakah (fatha, kasra, dama, tanwin) (Q5)		Ra Mutaharrikah, Sakinah (T17b,c)		Ra Mutaharrikah, Sakinah (T17b,c)		Revise, Identify Tajwid Rules T17b-T18c	
		Stretched Harakahs (stretch, lin) (Q6)		Full-Mouth Letters, Alif (T17d,e)		Full-Mouth Letters, Alif (T17d,e)		Reading Fluency: 15 Quran lines, 3 min	
		Joining Letters (sukun, shad), Madd (Q7,8)		Ikhfa, Idgham, Izhar Shafwi (T18a,b,c)		Ikhfa, Idgham, Izhar Shafwi (T18a,b,c)		Revise, Identify Tajwid Rules T19a-T20e	
		Special Cases, Fluency in 3 Words (Q9,10)		Qalb, Idgham w/o w Ghunnah (T19a,b,c)		Qalb, Idgham w/o w Ghunnah (T19a,b,c)			
		Stopping, Fluency in One Line (Q11,12,13)		Izhar, Ikhfa (T19d,e), Madd (T20a,b,c,d,e)		Izhar, Ikhfa (T19d,e), Madd (T20a,b,c,d,e)			
		All Makharij are Correct		Reading Fluency: 7 Quran lines, 3 min		Reading Fluency: 11 Quran lines, 3 min			
Quran Memorization		Surah Fatihah		Surah Fil		Surah 'Adiyat		Surah Inshirah*	
		Surah Ikhlas		Surah Quraish		Surah Qari'ah		Surah Tin*	
		Surah Falaq		Surah Ma'un		Surah Takathur		Surah Alaq*	
		Surah Nas		Surah Kawthar, Kafirun		Surah Asr		Surah Qadr*	
				Surah Nasr		Surah Humazah		Surah Bayyinah*	
				Surah Lahab				Surah Zilzal*	
Kalimah and Dua Memorization		First Kalimah with Meaning		Takbir Tahrima		Tashahhud		Qunut	
		Second Kalimah with Meaning		Dua Al -Istifta (Thana)				Dua to Make for Parent	
		Ta'awudh, Time Eating, Time Sleeping							
		Greeting Muslim, Reply to Salam		Tasbih of Ruku		Durud Ibrahim		Entering a House*	
		Drink Water, Hear Messenger (S) Name		Rising from Ruku		After Durud Ibrahim		Leaving a House*	
		We Sneeze, Other Sneezes, Reply Snzng*		In Qawmah		Before Wudu*		When Breaking the Fast	
		Entering Washroom, Leaving Washroom*		Tasbih of Sajdah		After Wudu		When Traveling	
		After Eating, Forget to Recite at Eating		Between Two Sajdah*		Entering the Masjid		Dua to Make for Host*	
		Waking Up		Completing the Salah		Leaving the Masjid*			
Islamic Studies				Intro 5 Pillars, Intro Taharah, Wudu Method (N1)		Cleaning Methods,Wudu Detail,Tayam Salah Method(N2)		NajasTyp,Ghusl,SalaRakt/Cond/Naw,Witr,Musaf,Mard(N3)	
				Feed Hungry, Help, Calmness, Purity, Truth (N1)*		Truth, Salam, Right Hand, Drink, Neighbors (N2)*		Salah,Love,Steadfst,Life,Dua,Guest,Mercy,Shukr(N3)*	
				Childhood, Youth, Marriage Khadijah, Children (N1)		Hira,Revelation,1st Believers,Open Call,Persecut(N2)		Abyssinia,Boycott,Year Sorrow,Taif,Invitation,Miraj(N3)	
				Adam (a), Nuh (a) (N1)		Hud (a), Salih (a) (N2)		Ibrahim (a), Ismail (a), Ishaq (a) (N3)	
				7 Articles, Who is Allah, Provider, Merciful (N1)		Protector, Hearer, Seer; One; Angel; Book; Quran (N2)		Messengers, Qiyamah, Minor Signs, Major Signs (N3)	
				Respect, Cleanliness, Polite, Smile, Right Side (N1)*		Promises, Thanking, Salam, Helping, Animals (N2)*		Thinking Good, Sharing, Parents, Truth, Good Word (N3)*	
				Eat, Drink, Sleeping, Waking, Washroom (N1)*		Greeting,Enter House, Speak, Sneeze, Yawn (N2)*		Traveling, Studying, Quran, Walking, Masjid (N3)*	

Scoring Key: ✓ Skill acquired prior to this year + Skill acquired this academic year <Blank> Skill not yet acquired or not tested / * Not required for students revising prior grades / Q Safar Qaidah Level, T Safar Tajwid Level, N Nasihah Grade

Adab✓Akhlaq✓aid Tark S✓raHadi Fiqh

Examiner Name & Date

Comments

Teachers: Complete and mark all scores and comments up to and including current grade, in pen. Examiners: Complete and mark only on top of scores marked by teachers, in thick pen. Add comments in pen.

Copyright © 2019 by Masjid Uthman (Uthman Academy, Uthman Seminary)

Comprehensive Assessment (Middle Grades)

Student: _____ Grade: _____ Year: 20___ - 20___

Subject		Grade 4		Grade 5		Grade 6		Grade 7	
	Skill	Skill	Score	Skill	Score	Skill	Score	Skill	Score
Quran Reading and Tajwid		Reading Fluency: 15 Quran lines, 3 min		Reading Fluency: 15 Quran lines, 2 min		Reading Fluency: 15 Quran lines, 2 min			
		Revise, Identify Tajwid Rules T14-T17a		Revise, Identify Tajwid Rules T14-T17a					
		Reading Fluency: 15 Quran lines, 2.5 min		Reading Fluency: 15 Quran lines, 2 min					
		Revise, Identify Tajwid Rules T17b-T18c		Revise, Identify Tajwid Rules T17b-T18c					
		Reading Fluency: 15 Quran lines, 2 min		Reading Fluency: 15 Quran lines, 2 min					
		Revise, Identify Tajwid Rules T19a-T20e		Revise, Identify Tajwid Rules T19a-T20e					
Quran Memorization		Surah Fajr*		Surah Yasin Ruku 1*		Surah Yasin Ruku 3*			
		Surah Balad*							
		Surah Shams*							
		Surah Layl*		Surah Yasin Ruku 2*		Surah Yasin Ruku 4*			
		Surah Dhuha*							
		Ayat Al-Kursi				Surah Yasin Ruku 5*			
Kalimah and Dua Memorization		Adhan		Protection from Calamities*		Returning from Journey*		Most Comprehensive Dua*	
		Extra Words for Fajr Adhan		At Conclusion of a Gathering				Talbiyah*	
		Reply to Words of Adhan*		When Visiting the Sick*		Protection from Evil Eye		Takbir of Tashriq	
		After Adhan*		When in Distress*		Sayyidul Istighfar		When Visiting Graveyard	
				When Feeling Anger*				Time of Burying Deceased*	
		Janazah Dua		Dua at Time of Need (Hajah)		When in Market Place*		To Benefit from Knowledge*	
		Janazah Dua Male Infant*		Dua on Laylatul Qadr*		When Having Nightmare		At the Time of Death*	
		Janazah Dua Female Infant*							
Islamic Studies (Adab Akhlaq Aqaid Tark Hadi Sirah Fiqh)		Khuff,Masah Wound,Salah Wajib,Sahw,Sawm,Taraw(N4)		Tayam,Salah Sunan,Salah Time,Masbuq,Qada,I.d,Haji(N5)		Water,I,mpur,Matur,I,mam,Salah Wajib,Janaiz,Jumah (N6)		Salah Makr,Saj Tilawa,Qasr,Zaka,I,nherit,Itkaf,Food(N7)	
		Feeding,Racism,Thank,Friend,Trust,Paradise,Zikr(N4)*		Promises,Tongue,Ghibah,Intox,99Names,Charact (N5)*		Major Sins,Pride,Health,Truth,Love Messeng,Parent (N6)*		People of Jann/Jahan, Ghibah, Modest,Salah Jamah (N7)*	
		Aqaba,Hijra,Treates,Hypocrit,Badr,Uhud,Ahzab(N4)		Hudaiba,Conquest Makkah,Hunain,Tabuk,Farewell (N5)		Shamail,Abu Bakr(r.),Life & Work, Mother Believers (N6)		Shamail, Umar(r.), Life and Work (N7)	
		Yaqub (a), Yusuf (a) (N4)		Musa (a), Isa (a) (N5)		Dawud (a), Sulayman (a), Yunus (a), Umayyads (N6)		Zakariyyah (a), Yahya, (a), Abbasids (N7)	
		Mahdi/Dajjal/Wajuj/Beast,Trumpet,Qiyama,Bridge(N4)		Death,Janna,Jahanam,Taqdir,Prophet/Khulafa,Allah/Prophet/Sahaba (N5)		Ahl Sunnah,Prophet,Khulafa,Ash Mubash,Mujiza (N6)		Qada and Qadr, Evil Eye, Life after Death, Barzakh (N7)	
		Trust, Permission Enter, Remov Harm, Neighbor (N4)*		Mashwara, Patience, Kinship, Gifts, Guest, Dhikr (N5)*		Oppression, Bullying, Envy, Ghibah, Pride, Sunnah (N6)*		Spreading Rumors, Value of Time, Knowledge, Durud (N7)*	
		Dua, Dress, Guest/Host, Gathering, Istinja (N4)*		Ghusl, Social Interaction, Writing, Siwak, Visit Sick (N5)*		Adhan, Modest Dress, Moderation Expend, Hygiene (N6)*		5 Branches,Faith, Oaths, Phone, Elders, Non-Muslims (N7)*	

Scoring Key: ✓ Skill acquired prior to this year + Skill acquired this academic year <Blank> Skill not yet acquired or not tested / Not required for students revising prior grades / Q Safar Qaidah Level, T Safar Tajwid Level, N Nasihah Grade

Examiner	
Name & Date	
Most Recent Comments	

Copyright © 2019 by Masjid Uthman (Uthman Academy, Uthman Seminary)

Teachers: Complete and mark all scores and comments up to and including current grade, in pen. **Examiners:** Complete and mark only on top of scores marked by teachers, in thick pen. Add comments in pen.

Comprehensive Assessment (Elementary Grades)

Student: _____ Grade: _____ Year: 20___ - 20___

Subject	Grade Qaidah Skill	Score	Grade 1 Skill	Score	Grade 2 Skill	Score	Grade 3 Skill	Score
Quran Reading and Tajwid	Pronunciation (alphabet) (Q1)		Ta'wudh, Mim Nun Mushadadah (T14,15)		Ta'wudh, Mim Nun Mushadadah (T14,15)		Reading Fluency: 11 Quran lines, 3 min	
	Letter Recognition (mixed, joined) (Q2)		Qalqalah (T16), Lam of Allah (T17a)		Qalqalah (T16), Lam of Allah (T17a)		Revise, Identify Tajwid Rules T14-T17a	
	Fluency Word, Adv Letter Recog (Q3,4)		Reading Fluency: 5 Quran lines, 3 min		Reading Fluency: 9 Quran lines, 3 min		Reading Fluency: 13 Quran lines, 3 min	
	Harakah (fatha, kasra, dama, tanwin) (Q5)		Ra Mutaharrikah, Sakinah (T17b,c)		Ra Mutaharrikah, Sakinah (T17b,c)		Revise, Identify Tajwid Rules T17b-T18c	
	Stretched Harakahs (stretch, lin) (Q6)		Full-Mouth Letters, Alif (T17d,e)		Full-Mouth Letters, Alif (T17d,e)			
	Joining Letters (sukun, shad), Madd (Q7,8)		Ikhfa, Idgham, Izhar Shafwi (T18a,b,c)		Ikhfa, Idgham, Izhar Shafwi (T18a,b,c)		Reading Fluency: 15 Quran lines, 3 min	
	Special Cases, Fluency in 3 Words (Q9,10)		Qalb, Idgham wo/w Ghunnah (T19a,b,c)		Qalb, Idgham wo/w Ghunnah (T19a,b,c)			
	Stopping, Fluency in One Line (Q11,12,13)		Izhar, Ikhfa (T19d,e), Madd (T20a,b,c,d,e)		Izhar, Ikhfa (T19d,e), Madd (T20a,b,c,d,e)		Revise, Identify Tajwid Rules T19a-T20e	
	All Makharij are Correct		Reading Fluency: 7 Quran lines, 3 min		Reading Fluency: 11 Quran lines, 3 min			
Quran Memorization	Surah Fatihah		Surah Fil		Surah 'Adiyat		Surah Inshirah*	
			Surah Quraish				Surah Tin*	
	Surah Ikhlas		Surah Ma'un		Surah Qari'ah		Surah Alaq*	
	Surah Falaq		Surah Kawthar, Kafirun		Surah Takathur		Surah Qadr*	
	Surah Nas		Surah Nasr		Surah Asr		Surah Bayyinah*	
			Surah Lahab		Surah Humazah		Surah Zilzal*	
Kalimah and Dua Memorization	First Kalimah with Meaning		Takbir Tahrima		Tashahhud		Qunut	
	Second Kalimah with Meaning		Dua Al-Istifta (Thana)				Dua to Make for Parent	
	Ta'awudh, Time Eating, Time Sleeping							
	Greeting Muslim, Reply to Salam		Tasbih of Ruku		Durud Ibrahim		Entering a House*	
	Drink Water, Hear Messenger (S) Name		Rising from Ruku		After Durud Ibrahim		Leaving a House*	
	We Sneeze, Other Sneezes, Reply Snzng*		In Qawmah		Before Wudu*		When Breaking the Fast	
	Entering Washroom, Leaving Washroom*		Tasbih of Sajdah		After Wudu		When Traveling	
	After Eating, Forget to Recite at Eating		Between Two Sajdah*		Entering the Masjid		Dua to Make for Host*	
	Waking Up		Completing the Salah		Leaving the Masjid*			
Islamic Studies			Intro 5 Pillars, Intro Taharah, Wudu Method (N1)		Cleaning Methods, Wudu Detail, Tayam Salah Method (N2)		Najas Typ, Ghusl, SalaRakt/Cond/Naw, Witr, Musaf Mard (N3)	
			Feed Hungy, Help, Calmness, Purity, Truth (N1)*		Truth, Salam, Right Hand, Drink, Neighbors (N2)*		Salah, Love, Steadfst, Life, Dua, Guest, Mercy, Shukr (N3)*	
			Childhood, Youth, Marriage Khadijah, Children (N1)		Hira, Revelation, 1st Believers, Open Call, Persecut (N2)		Abysinia, Boycott, Year Sorrow, Taif, Invitation, Miraj (N3)	
			Adam (a), Nuh (a) (N1)		Hud (a), Salih (a) (N2)		Ibrahim (a), Ismail (a), Ishaq (a) (N3)	
			7 Articles, Who is Allah, Provider, Merciful (N1)		Protector, Hearer, Seer, One; Angel; Book; Quran (N2)		Messengers, Qyamah, Minor Signs, Major Signs (N3)	
			Respect, Cleanliness, Polite, Smile, Right Side (N1)*		Promises, Thanking, Salam, Helping, Animals (N2)*		Thinking Good, Sharing, Parents, Truth, Good Word (N3)*	
			Eat, Drink, Sleeping, Waking, Washroom (N1)*		Greeting, Enter House, Speak, Sneeze, Yawn (N2)*		Traveling, Studying, Quran, Waking, Masjid (N3)*	

Adab/Akhlq Aqaid Tarik Sirat Hadi Fiqh

Scoring Key: ✓ Skill acquired prior to this year + Skill acquired this academic year <Blank> Skill not yet acquired or not tested / * Not required for students revising prior grades / Q Safar Qaidah Level, T Safar Tajwid Level, N Nasihah Grade

Examiner		
Name & Date		
Comments		

Copyright © 2019 by Masjid Uthman (Uthman Academy, Uthman Seminary)

Teachers: Complete and mark all scores and comments up to and including current grade, in pen. **Examiners:** Complete and mark only on top of scores marked by teachers, in thick pen. Add comments in pen.

Comprehensive Assessment (Middle Grades)

Student: _____ Grade: _____ Year: 20____ - 20____

Subject	Grade 4 Skill	Score	Grade 5 Skill	Score	Grade 6 Skill	Score	Grade 7 Skill	Score
Quran Reading and Tajwid	Reading Fluency: 15 Quran lines, 3 min		Reading Fluency: 15 Quran lines, 2 min					
	Revise, Identify Tajwid Rules T14-T17a		Revise, Identify Tajwid Rules T14-T17a					
	Reading Fluency: 15 Quran lines, 2.5 min		Reading Fluency: 15 Quran lines, 2 min					
	Revise, Identify Tajwid Rules T17b-T18c		Revise, Identify Tajwid Rules T17b-T18c					
	Reading Fluency: 15 Quran lines, 2 min		Reading Fluency: 15 Quran lines, 2 min					
	Revise, Identify Tajwid Rules T19a-T20e		Revise, Identify Tajwid Rules T19a-T20e					
Quran Memorization	Surah Fajr*		Surah Yasin Ruku 1*		Surah Yasin Ruku 3*			
	Surah Balad*							
	Surah Shams*							
	Surah Layl*		Surah Yasin Ruku 2*		Surah Yasin Ruku 4*			
	Surah Dhuha*							
	Ayat Al-Kursi				Surah Yasin Ruku 5*			
Kalimah and Dua Memorization	Adhan		Protection from Calamities*				Most Comprehensive Dua*	
	Extra Words for Fajr Adhan		At Conclusion of a Gathering		Returning from Journey*		Talbiyah*	
	Reply to Words of Adhan*		When Visiting the Sick*		Protection from Evil Eye		Takbir of Tashriq*	
	After Adhan*		When in Distress*		Sayyidul Istighfar		When Visiting Graveyard	
	Janazah Dua		When Feeling Anger*		When in Market Place*		Time of Burying Deceased*	
	Janazah Dua Male Infant*		Dua at Time of Need (Hajah)		When Having Nightmare		To Benefit from Knowledge*	
	Janazah Dua Female Infant*		Dua on Laylatul Qadr*				At the Time of Death*	
Islamic Studies	Khuff,Masah Wound,Salah Wajib,Sahw,Sawm,Taraw(N4)		Tayam,Salah Sunan,Salah Time,Masbuq,Qada,Id,Hajj(N5)		Water,Impur,Matur,Imam,Salah Wajib,Janaiz,Jumah (N6)		Salah Makr,Saj Tilawa,Qasr,Zaka,Inherit,Itikaf,Food(N7)	
	Feeding,Racism,Thank,Friend,Trust,Paradise,Zikr(N4)*		Promises,Tongue,Ghibah,Intox,99Names,Charact (N5)*		Major Sins,Pride,Health,Truth,Love Messeng,Parent (N6)*		People of Jann/Jahan,Ghibah, Modest,Salah Jamah (N7)*	
	Aqaba,Hijra,Treaties,Hypocrit,Badr,Uhud,Ahzab(N4)		Hudaibia,Conquest Makkah,Hunain,Tabuk,Farewell (N5)		Shamail, Abu Bakr (r), Life & Work, Mother Believers (N6)		Shamail, Umar (r), Life and Work (N7)	
	Yaqub(a), Yusuf (a) (N4)		Musa (a), Isa (a) (N5)		Dawud (a), Sulayman (a), Yunus (a), Umayyads (N6)		Zakariyyah (a), Yahya, (a), Abbasids (N7)	
	Mahdi/Dajal/Yajuj/Beast,Trumpet,Qiyama,Bridge(N4)		Death,Janna,Jahanam,Taqdir, Allah/Prophet/Sahaba (N5)		Ahl Sunnah,Prophet,Khulafa,Ash Mubash,Mujiza (N6)		Qada and Qadr, Evil Eye, Life after Death, Barzakh (N7)	
	Trust, Permission Enter, Remov Harm, Neighbor (N4)*		Mashwara, Patience, Kinship, Gifts, Guest, Dhikr (N5)*		Oppression, Bullying, Envy, Ghibah, Pride, Sunnah (N6)*		Spreading Rumors, Value of Time, Knowledge, Durud (N7)*	
	Dua, Dress, Guest/Host, Gathering, Istinja (N4)*		Ghusl, Social Interaction, Writing, Siwak, Visit Sick (N5)*		Adhan, Modest Dress, Moderation Expend, Hygiene (N6)*		5 Branches Faith, Oaths, Phone, Elders, Non-Muslims (N7)*	

Rows (Islamic Studies subcategories, bottom to top along left margin): Adab Akhlaq, Aqaid, Tark, Sirah, Hadi, Fiqh

Scoring Key: ✓ Skill acquired prior to this year + Skill acquired this academic year <Blank> Skill not yet acquired or not tested / * Not required for students revising prior grades / **Q** Safar Qaidah Level, **T** Safar Tajwid Level, **N** Nasihah Grade

Examiner				
Name & Date				
Most Recent Comments				

Copyright © 2019 by Masjid Uthman (Uthman Academy, Uthman Seminary)

Teachers: Complete and mark all scores and comments up to and including current grade, in pen. **Examiners:** Complete and mark only on top of scores marked by teachers, in thick pen. Add comments in pen.

Comprehensive Assessment (Elementary Grades)

Subject: _____ Student: _____ Grade: _____ Year: 20___ - 20___

Subject	Grade Qaidah Skill	Score	Grade 1 Skill	Score	Grade 2 Skill	Score	Grade 3 Skill	Score
Quran Reading and Tajwid	Pronunciation (alphabet) (Q1)		Ta'wudh, Mim Nun Mushadadah (T14,15)		Ta'wudh, Mim Nun Mushadadah (T14,15)		Reading Fluency: 11 Quran lines, 3 min	
	Letter Recognition (mixed, joined) (Q2)		Qalqalah (T16), Lam of Allah (T17a)		Qalqalah (T16), Lam of Allah (T17a)		Revise, Identify Tajwid Rules T14-T17a	
	Fluency Word, Adv Letter Recog (Q3,4)		Reading Fluency: 5 Quran lines, 3 min		Reading Fluency: 9 Quran lines, 3 min		Reading Fluency: 13 Quran lines, 3 min	
	Harakah (fatha, kasra, dama, tanwin) (Q5)		Ra Mutaharrikah, Sakinah (T17b,c)		Ra Mutaharrikah, Sakinah (T17b,c)		Revise, Identify Tajwid Rules T17b-T18c	
	Stretched Harakahs (stretch, lin) (Q6)		Full-Mouth Letters, Alif (T17d,e)		Full-Mouth Letters, Alif (T17d,e)		Reading Fluency: 15 Quran lines, 3 min	
	Joining Letters (sukun, shad), Madd (Q7,8)		Ikhfa, Idgham, Izhar Shafwi (T18a,b,c)		Ikhfa, Idgham, Izhar Shafwi (T18a,b,c)		Revise, Identify Tajwid Rules T19a-T20e	
	Special Cases, Fluency in 3 Words (Q9,10)		Qalb, Idgham wo/w Ghunnah (T19a,b,c)		Qalb, Idgham wo/w Ghunnah (T19a,b,c)			
	Stopping, Fluency in One Line (Q11,12,13)		Izhar, Ikhfa (T19d,e), Madd (T20a,b,c,d,e)		Izhar, Ikhfa (T19d,e), Madd (T20a,b,c,d,e)			
	All Makharij are Correct		Reading Fluency: 7 Quran lines, 3 min		Reading Fluency: 11 Quran lines, 3 min			
Quran Memorization	Surah Fatihah		Surah Fil		Surah 'Adiyat		Surah Inshirah*	
	Surah Ikhlas		Surah Quraish		Surah Qari'ah		Surah Tin*	
	Surah Falaq		Surah Ma'un		Surah Takathur		Surah Alaq*	
	Surah Nas		Surah Kawthar, Kafirun		Surah Asr		Surah Qadr*	
			Surah Nasr		Surah Humazah		Surah Bayyinah*	
			Surah Lahab				Surah Zilzal*	
Kalimah and Dua Memorization	First Kalimah with Meaning		Takbir Tahrima		Tashahhud		Qunut	
	Second Kalimah with Meaning		Dua Al-Istifta (Thana)				Dua to Make for Parent	
	Ta'awudh, Time Eating, Time Sleeping							
	Greeting Muslim, Reply to Salam		Tasbih of Ruku		Durud Ibrahim		Entering a House*	
	Drink Water, Hear Messenger (S) Name		Rising from Ruku		After Durud Ibrahim*		Leaving a House*	
	We Sneeze, Other Sneezes, Reply Snzng*		In Qawmah		Before Wudu*		When Breaking the Fast	
	Entering Washroom, Leaving Washroom*		Tasbih of Sajdah		After Wudu		When Traveling	
	After Eating, Forget to Recite at Eating		Between Two Sajdah*		Entering the Masjid		Dua to Make for Host*	
	Waking Up		Completing the Salah		Leaving the Masjid*			
Islamic Studies			Intro 5 Pillars, Intro Taharah, Wudu Method (N1)		Cleaning Methods, Wudu Detail, Tayam Salah Method (N2)		Najas Typ, Ghusl, Sala Rakt/Cond/Naw, Witr, Musaf, Mard (N3)	
			Feed Hungry, Help, Calmness, Purity, Truth (N1)*		Truth, Salam, Right Hand, Drink, Neighbors (N2)*		Salah, Love, Steadfst, Life, Dua, Guest, Mercy, Shukr (N3)*	
			Childhood, Youth, Marriage Khadijah, Children (N1)		Hira, Revelation, 1st Believers, Open Call, Persecut (N2)		Abyssinia, Boycott, Year Sorrow, Taif, Invitation, Miraj (N3)	
			Adam (a), Nuh (a) (N1)		Hud (a), Salih (a) (N2)		Ibrahim (a), Ismail (a), Ishaq (a) (N3)	
			7 Articles, Who is Allah, Provider, Merciful (N1)		Protector, Hearer, Seer, One; Angel; Book; Quran (N2)		Messengers, Qiyamah, Minor Signs, Major Signs (N3)	
			Respect, Cleanliness, Polite, Smile, Right Side (N1)*		Promises, Thanking, Salam, Helping, Animals (N2)*		Thinking Good, Sharing, Parents, Truth, Good Word (N3)*	
			Eat, Drink, Sleeping, Waking, Washroom (N1)*		Greeting, Enter House, Speak, Sneeze, Yawn (N2)*		Traveling, Studying, Quran, Walking, Masjid (N3)*	

Adab Akhlaq (Aqaid) Tarik Sirah Hadith Fiqh

Scoring Key: ✓ Skill acquired prior to this year + Skill acquired this academic year <Blank> Skill not yet acquired or not tested / * Not required for students revising prior grades / Q Safar Qaidah Level, T Safar Tajwid Level, N Nasihah Grade

Examiner Name & Date: _____

Comments: _____

Teachers: Complete and mark all scores and comments up to and including current grade, in pen. Examiners: Complete and mark only on top of scores marked by teachers, in thick pen. Add comments in pen.

Copyright © 2019 by Masjid Uthman (Uthman Academy, Uthman Seminary)

Comprehensive Assessment (Middle Grades)

Student: _____ Grade: _____ Year: 20___ - 20___

Subject	Grade 4 Skill	Score	Grade 5 Skill	Score	Grade 6 Skill	Score	Grade 7 Skill	Score
Quran Reading and Tajwid	Reading Fluency: 15 Quran lines, 3 min		Reading Fluency: 15 Quran lines, 2 min					
	Revise, Identify Tajwid Rules T14-T17a		Revise, Identify Tajwid Rules T14-T17a					
	Reading Fluency: 15 Quran lines, 2.5 min		Reading Fluency: 15 Quran lines, 2 min					
	Revise, Identify Tajwid Rules T17b-T18c		Revise, Identify Tajwid Rules T17b-T18c					
	Reading Fluency: 15 Quran lines, 2 min		Reading Fluency: 15 Quran lines, 2 min					
	Revise, Identify Tajwid Rules T19a-T20e		Revise, Identify Tajwid Rules T19a-T20e					
Quran Memorization	Surah Fajr*		Surah Yasin Ruku 1*		Surah Yasin Ruku 3*			
	Surah Balad*							
	Surah Shams*							
	Surah Layl*		Surah Yasin Ruku 2*		Surah Yasin Ruku 4*			
	Surah Dhuha*							
	Ayat Al-Kursi				Surah Yasin Ruku 5*			
Kalimah and Dua Memorization	Adhan		Protection from Calamities*		Returning from Journey*		Most Comprehensive Dua*	
	Extra Words for Fajr Adhan		At Conclusion of a Gathering				Talbiyah*	
	Reply to Words of Adhan*		When Visiting the Sick*		Protection from Evil Eye		Takbir of Tashriq*	
	After Adhan*		When in Distress*		Sayyidul Istighfar		When Visiting Graveyard	
			When Feeling Anger*				Time of Burying Deceased*	
	Janazah Dua		Dua at Time of Need (Hajah)		When in Market Place*		To Benefit from Knowledge*	
	Janazah Dua Male Infant*		Dua on Laylatul Qadr*		When Having Nightmare		At the Time of Death*	
	Janazah Dua Female Infant*							
Islamic Studies	Khuff,Masah Wound,Salah Wajib,Sahw,Sawm,Taraw(N4)		Tayam,Salah Sunan,Salah Time,Masbuq,Qada,Id,Hajj(N5)		Water,Impur,Matur,Imam,Salah Wajib,Janaiz,Jumah (N6)		Salah Makr,Saj,Tilawa,Qasr,Zaka,Inherit,Itikaf,Food(N7)	
	Feeding,Racism,Thank,Friend,Trust,Paradise,Zikr(N4)*		Promises,Tongue,Ghibah,Intox,99Names, Charact (N5)*		Major Sins,Pride,Health,Truth,Love Messeng,Parent (N6)*		PeopleofJann/Jahan, Ghibah, Modest,Salah Jamah (N7)*	
	Aqaba,Hijra,Treaties,Hypocrit,Badr,Uhud,Ahzab(N4)		Hudaibia,Conquest Makkah,Hunain,Tabuk,Farewell(N5)		Shamail,Abu Bakr (r.), Life & Work, Mother Believers (N6)		Shamail,Umar (r.), Life and Work (N7)	
	Yaqub (a), Yusuf (a) (N4)		Musa (a), Isa (a) (N5)		Dawud (a), Sulayman (a), Yunus (a), Umayyads (N6)		Zakariyyah (a), Yahya, (a), Abbasids (N7)	
	Mahdi/Dajjal/Yajuj/Beast,Trumpet,Qiyama,Bridge(N4)		Death,Janna,Jahanam,Taqdir, Allah/Prophet/Sahaba (N5)		Ahl Sunnah,Prophet,Khulafa, Ash Mubash,Mujiza (N6)		Qada and Qadr, Evil Eye, Life after Death, Barzakh (N7)	
	Trust, Permission Enter, Remov Harm, Neighbor (N4)*		Mashwara, Patience, Kinship, Gifts, Guest, Dhikr (N5)*		Oppression, Bullying, Envy, Ghibah, Pride, Sunnah (N6)*		Spreading Rumors, Value of Time, Knowledge, Durud (N7)*	
	Dua, Dress, Guest/Host, Gathering, Istinja (N4)*		Ghusl, Social Interaction, Writing, Siwak, Visit Sick (N5)*		Adhan, Modest Dress, Moderation Expend, Hygiene (N6)*		5 Branches,Faith, Oaths, Phone, Elders, Non-Muslims (N7)*	

Adab Akhlaq Aqaid Tark Hadi Sirah Fiqh

Scoring Key: ✓ Skill acquired prior to this year + Skill acquired this academic year <Blank> Skill not yet acquired or not tested / * Not required for students revising prior grades / Q Safar Qaidah Level, T Safar Tajwid Level, N Nasihah Grade

Examiner Name & Date	
Most Recent Comments	

Copyright © 2019 by Masjid Uthman (Uthman Academy, Uthman Seminary)

Teachers: Complete and mark all scores and comments up to and including current grade, in pen. **Examiners:** Complete and mark only on top of scores marked by teachers, in thick pen. Add comments in pen.

Comprehensive Assessment (Elementary Grades)

Grade: _____   Student: _____   Year: 20___ - 20___   Grade: _____

Subject		Grade Qaidah		Grade 1		Grade 2		Grade 3	
		Skill	Score	Skill	Score	Skill	Score	Skill	Score
Quran Reading and Tajwid		Pronunciation (alphabet) (Q1)		Ta'wudh, Mim Nun Mushadadah (T14,15)		Ta'wudh, Mim Nun Mushadadah (T14,15)		Reading Fluency: 11 Quran lines, 3 min	
		Letter Recognition (mixed, joined) (Q2)		Qalqalah (T16), Lam of Allah (T17a)		Qalqalah (T16), Lam of Allah (T17a)		Revise, Identify Tajwid Rules T14-T17a	
		Fluency Word, Adv Letter Recog (Q3,4)		Reading Fluency: 5 Quran lines, 3 min		Reading Fluency: 9 Quran lines, 3 min		Reading Fluency: 13 Quran lines, 3 min	
		Harakah (fatha, kasra, dama, tanwin) (Q5)		Ra Mutaharrikah, Sakinah (T17b,c)		Ra Mutaharrikah, Sakinah (T17b,c)		Revise, Identify Tajwid Rules T17b-T18c	
		Stretched Harakahs (stretch, lin) (Q6)		Full-Mouth Letters, Alif (T17d,e)		Full-Mouth Letters, Alif (T17d,e)		Reading Fluency: 15 Quran lines, 3 min	
		Joining Letters (sukun, shad), Madd (Q7,8)		Ikhfa, Idgham, Izhar Shafwi (T18a,b,c)		Ikhfa, Idgham, Izhar Shafwi (T18a,b,c)		Revise, Identify Tajwid Rules T19a-T20e	
		Special Cases, Fluency in 3 Words (Q9,10)		Qalb, Idgham wo/w Ghunnah (T19a,b,c)		Qalb, Idgham wo/w Ghunnah (T19a,b,c)			
		Stopping, Fluency in One Line (Q11,12,13)		Izhar, Ikhfa (T19d,e), Madd (T20a,b,c,d,e)		Izhar, Ikhfa (T19d,e), Madd (T20a,b,c,d,e)			
		All Makharij are Correct		Reading Fluency: 7 Quran lines, 3 min		Reading Fluency: 11 Quran lines, 3 min			
Quran Memorization		Surah Fatihah		Surah Fil		Surah 'Adiyat		Surah Inshirah*	
		Surah Ikhlas		Surah Quraish		Surah Qari'ah		Surah Tin*	
		Surah Falaq		Surah Ma'un		Surah Takathur		Surah Alaq*	
		Surah Nas		Surah Kawthar, Kafirun		Surah Asr		Surah Qadr*	
				Surah Nasr		Surah Humazah		Surah Bayyinah*	
				Surah Lahab				Surah Zilzal*	
Kalimah and Dua Memorization		First Kalimah with Meaning		Takbir Tahrima		Tashahhud		Qunut	
		Second Kalimah with Meaning		Dua Al-Istifta (Thana)				Dua to Make for Parent	
		Ta'awudh, Time Eating, Time Sleeping							
		Greeting Muslim, Reply to Salam		Tasbih of Ruku		Durud Ibrahim		Entering a House*	
		Drink Water, Hear Messenger (S) Name		Rising from Ruku		After Durud Ibrahim		Leaving a House*	
		We Sneeze, Other Sneezes, Reply Snzng*		In Qawmah		Before Wudu*		When Breaking the Fast	
		Entering Washroom, Leaving Washroom*		Tasbih of Sajdah		After Wudu		When Traveling	
		After Eating, Forget to Recite at Eating		Between Two Sajdah*		Entering the Masjid		Dua to Make for Host*	
		Waking Up		Completing the Salah		Leaving the Masjid*			
Islamic Studies				Intro 5 Pillars, Intro Taharah, Wudu Method (N1)		Cleaning Methods,Wudu Detail,Tayam,Salah Method(N2)		Najas Typ,Ghusl,SabaRakt/Cond/Naw,Witr,Musaf,Mard(N3)	
				Feed Hungry, Help, Calmness, Purity, Truth (N1)*		Truth, Salam, Right Hand, Drink, Neighbors (N2)*		Salah,Love,Steadfast,Life,Dua,Guest,Mercy,Shukr(N3)*	
				Childhood, Youth, Marriage Khadijah, Children (N1)		Hira,Revelation,1st Believers,Open Call,Persecut(N2)		Abyssinia,Boycott,Year Sorrow,Taif,Invitation,Miraj(N3)	
				Adam (a), Nuh (a) (N1)		Hud (a), Salih (a) (N2)		Ibrahim (a), Ismail (a), Ishaq (a) (N3)	
				7 Articles, Who is Allah, Provider, Merciful (N1)		Protector, Hearer, Seer, One; Angel; Book; Quran (N2)		Messengers, Qiyamah, Minor Signs, Major Signs (N3)	
				Respect, Cleanliness, Polite, Smile, Right Side (N1)*		Promises, Thanking, Salam, Helping, Animals (N2)*		Thinking Good, Sharing, Parents, Truth, Good Word (N3)*	
				Eat, Drink, Sleeping, Waking, Washroom (N1)*		Greeting, Enter House, Speak, Sneeze, Yawn (N2)*		Traveling, Studying, Quran, Walking, Masjid (N3)*	

Subject labels (side): Adab Akhlaq, Qaidah, Tarikh, Sirah, Hadi, Fiqh

Scoring Key: ✔ Skill acquired prior to this year + Skill acquired this academic year <Blank> Skill not yet acquired or not tested / * Not required for students revising prior grades / **Q** Safar Qaidah Level, **T** Safar Tajwid Level, **N** Nasihah Grade

Examiner Name & Date:

Comments:

Copyright © 2019 by Masjid Uthman (Uthman Academy, Uthman Seminary)

Teachers: Complete and mark all scores and comments up to and including current grade, in pen. **Examiners:** Complete and mark only on top of scores marked by teachers, in thick pen. Add comments in pen.

Comprehensive Assessment (Middle Grades)

Student: _____ Grade: _____ Year: 20____ - 20____

Subject	Grade 4		Grade 5		Grade 6		Grade 7	
	Skill	Score	Skill	Score	Skill	Score	Skill	Score
Quran Reading and Tajwid	Reading Fluency: 15 Quran lines, 3 min		Reading Fluency: 15 Quran lines, 2 min					
	Revise, Identify Tajwid Rules T14-T17a		Revise, Identify Tajwid Rules T14-T17a					
	Reading Fluency: 15 Quran lines, 2.5 min		Reading Fluency: 15 Quran lines, 2 min					
	Revise, Identify Tajwid Rules T17b-T18c		Revise, Identify Tajwid Rules T17b-T18c					
	Reading Fluency: 15 Quran lines, 2 min		Reading Fluency: 15 Quran lines, 2 min					
	Revise, Identify Tajwid Rules T19a-T20e		Revise, Identify Tajwid Rules T19a-T20e					
Quran Memorization	Surah Fajr*		Surah Yasin Ruku 1*		Surah Yasin Ruku 3*			
	Surah Balad*							
	Surah Shams*							
	Surah Layl*		Surah Yasin Ruku 2*		Surah Yasin Ruku 4*			
	Surah Dhuha*							
	Ayat Al-Kursi				Surah Yasin Ruku 5*			
Kalimah and Dua Memorization	Adhan		Protection from Calamities*				Most Comprehensive Dua*	
	Extra Words for Fajr Adhan		At Conclusion of a Gathering		Returning from Journey*		Talbiyah*	
	Reply to Words of Adhan*		When Visiting the Sick*		Protection from Evil Eye		Takbir of Tashriq*	
	After Adhan*		When in Distress*		Sayyidul Istighfar		When Visiting Graveyard	
	Janazah Dua		When Feeling Anger*		When in Market Place*		Time of Burying Deceased*	
	Janazah Dua Male Infant*		Dua at Time of Need (Hajah)		When Having Nightmare		To Benefit from Knowledge*	
	Janazah Dua Female Infant*		Dua on Laylatul Qadr*				At the Time of Death*	
Islamic Studies	Khuff,Masah Wound,Salah Wajib,Sahw,Sawm,Taraw(N4)		Tayam,Salah Sunan,Salah Time,Masbuq,Qada,I,d.Hajj(N5)		Water,Impur,Matur,Imam,Salah Wajib,Janaiz,Jumah (N6)		Salah Makr,Saj,Tilawa,Qasr,Zaka,Inherit,Itikaf,Food(N7)	
	Feeding,Racism,Thank,Friend,Trust,Paradise,Zikr(N4)		Promises,Tongue,Ghibah,Intox,99Names,Charact (N5)*		Major Sins,Pride,Health,Truth,Love Messeng,Parent (N6)*		PeopleofJann/Jahan, Ghibah, Modest, Salah Jamah (N7)*	
	Aqaba,Hijra,Treaties,Hypocrit,Badr,Uhud,Ahzab(N4)		Hudaibia,Conquest Makkah,Hunain,Tabuk,Farewell(N5)		Shamail,Abu Bakr (r), Life & Work, Mother Believers (N6)		Shamail, Umar (r), Life and Work (N7)	
	Yaqub (a), Yusuf (a) (N4)		Musa (a), Isa (a) (N5)		Dawud (a), Sulayman (a), Yunus (a), Umayyads (N6)		Zakariyyah (a), Yahya, (a) , Abbasids (N7)	
	Mahdi/Dajjal/Yajuj/Beast,Trumpet,Qiyama,Bridge(N4)		Death,Janna,Jahanam,Taqdir, Allah/Prophet/Sahaba (N5)		Ahl Sunnah,Prophet,Khulafa,Ash Mubash,Mujiza (N6)		Qada and Qadr, Evil Eye, Life after Death, Barzakh (N7)	
	Trust, Permission Enter, Remov Harm, Neighbor (N4)*		Mashwara, Patience, Kinship, Gifts, Guest, Dhikr (N5)*		Oppression, Bullying, Envy, Ghibah, Pride, Sunnah (N6)*		Spreading Rumors, Value of Time, Knowledge, Durud (N7)*	
	Dua, Dress, Guest/Host, Gathering, Istinja (N4)*		Ghusl, Social Interaction, Writing, Swak, Visit Sick (N5)*		Adhan, Modest Dress, Moderation Expend, Hygiene (N6)*		5 Branches Faith, Oaths, Phone, Elders, Non-Muslims (N7)*	

Subject category labels (left margin, vertical): Adab, Akhlaq, Aqaid, Tark, Sirah, Hadi, Fiqh

Scoring Key: ✓ Skill acquired prior to this year + Skill acquired this year <Blank> Skill not yet acquired or not tested / * Not required for students revising prior grades / **Q** Safar Qaidah Level, **T** Safar Tajwid Level, **N** Nasihah Grade

Examiner	
Name & Date	
Most Recent Comments	

Teachers: Complete and mark all scores and comments up to and including current grade, in pen. Examiners: Complete and mark only on top of scores marked by teachers, in thick pen. Add comments in pen.

Copyright © 2019 by Masjid Uthman (Uthman Academy, Uthman Seminary)

Comprehensive Assessment (Elementary Grades)

Student: _____ Grade: _____ Year: 20___ - 20___

Subject		Grade Qaidah		Grade 1		Grade 2		Grade 3	
		Skill	Score	Skill	Score	Skill	Score	Skill	Score
Quran Reading and Tajwid		Pronunciation (alphabet) (Q1)		Ta'wudh, Mim Nun Mushadadah (T14,15)		Ta'wudh, Mim Nun Mushadadah (T14,15)		Reading Fluency: 11 Quran lines, 3 min	
		Letter Recognition (mixed, joined) (Q2)		Qalqalah (T16), Lam of Allah (T17a)		Qalqalah (T16), Lam of Allah (T17a)		Revise, Identify Tajwid Rules T14-T17a	
		Fluency Word, Adv Letter Recog (Q3,4)		Reading Fluency: 5 Quran lines, 3 min		Reading Fluency: 9 Quran lines, 3 min		Reading Fluency: 13 Quran lines, 3 min	
		Harakah (fatha, kasra, dama, tanwin) (Q5)		Ra Mutaharrikah, Sakinah (T17b,c)		Ra Mutaharrikah, Sakinah (T17b,c)			
		Stretched Harakahs (stretch, lin) (Q6)		Full-Mouth Letters, Alif (T17d,e)		Full-Mouth Letters, Alif (T17d,e)			
		Joining Letters (sukun, shad), Madd (Q7,8)		Ikhfa, Idgham, Izhar Shafwi (T18a,b,c)		Ikhfa, Idgham, Izhar Shafwi (T18a,b,c)		Revise, Identify Tajwid Rules T17b-T18c	
		Special Cases, Fluency in 3 Words (Q9,10)		Qalb, Idgham wo/w Ghunnah (T19a,b,c)		Qalb, Idgham wo/w Ghunnah (T19a,b,c)		Reading Fluency: 15 Quran lines, 3 min	
		Stopping, Fluency in One Line (Q11,12,13)		Izhar, Ikhfa (T19d,e), Madd (T20a,b,c,d,e)		Izhar, Ikhfa (T19d,e), Madd (T20a,b,c,d,e)			
		All Makharij are Correct		Reading Fluency: 7 Quran lines, 3 min		Reading Fluency: 11 Quran lines, 3 min		Revise, Identify Tajwid Rules T19a-T20e	
Quran Memorization		Surah Fatihah		Surah Fil		Surah 'Adiyat		Surah Inshirah*	
		Surah Ikhlas		Surah Quraish				Surah Tin*	
		Surah Falaq		Surah Ma'un		Surah Qari'ah		Surah Alaq*	
		Surah Nas		Surah Kawthar, Kafirun		Surah Takathur		Surah Qadr*	
				Surah Nasr		Surah Asr		Surah Bayyinah*	
				Surah Lahab		Surah Humazah		Surah Zilzal*	
Kalimah and Dua Memorization		First Kalimah with Meaning		Takbir Tahrima		Tashahhud		Qunut	
		Second Kalimah with Meaning		Dua Al-Istifta (Thana)				Dua to Make for Parent	
		Ta'awudh, Time Eating, Time Sleeping							
		Greeting Muslim, Reply to Salam		Tasbih of Ruku		Durud Ibrahim		Entering a House*	
		Drink Water, Hear Messenger (S) Name		Rising from Ruku		After Durud Ibrahim		Leaving a House*	
		We Sneeze, Other Sneezes, Reply Snzng*		In Qawmah		Before Wudu*		When Breaking the Fast	
		Entering Washroom, Leaving Washroom*		Tasbih of Sajdah		After Wudu		When Traveling	
		After Eating, Forget to Recite at Eating		Between Two Sajdah*		Entering the Masjid		Dua to Make for Host*	
		Waking Up		Completing the Salah		Leaving the Masjid*			
Islamic Studies				Intro 5 Pillars, Intro Taharah, Wudu Method (N1)		Cleaning Methods, Wudu Detail, Tayam, Salah Method (N2)		Najas Typ, Ghusl, Sala Rakt/Cond/Naw, Witr, Musaf, Mard (N3)	
				Feed Hungry, Help, Calmness, Purity, Truth (N1)*		Truth, Salam, Right Hand, Drink, Neighbors (N2)*		Salah, Love, Steadfst, Life, Dua, Guest, Mercy, Shukr (N3)*	
				Childhood, Youth, Marriage Khadijah, Children (N1)		Hira, Revelation, 1st Believers, Open Call, Persecut (N2)		Abyssinia, Boycott, Year Sorrow, Taif, Invitation, Miraj (N3)	
				Adam (a), Nuh (a) (N1)		Hud (a), Salih (a) (N2)		Ibrahim (a), Ismail (a), Ishaq (a) (N3)	
				7 Articles, Who is Allah, Provider, Merciful (N1)		Protector, Hearer, Seer, One; Angel; Book; Quran (N2)		Messengers, Qiyamah, Minor Signs, Major Signs (N3)	
				Respect, Cleanliness, Polite, Smile, Right Side (N1)*		Promises, Thanking, Salam, Helping, Animals (N2)*		Thinking Good, Sharing, Parents, Truth, Good Word (N3)*	
				Eat, Drink, Sleeping, Waking, Washroom (N1)*		Greeting, Enter House, Speak, Sneeze, Yawn (N2)*		Traveling, Studying, Quran, Walking, Masjid (N3)*	

Adab/Akhlaq/Aqaid/Tarikh/Sirah/Hadith/Fiqh

Scoring Key: ✓ Skill acquired prior to this year + Skill acquired this academic year <Blank> Skill not yet acquired or not tested / * Not required for students revising prior grades / **Q** Safar Qaidah Level, **T** Safar Tajwid Level, **N** Nasihah Grade

Examiner Name & Date: _____

Comments: _____

Copyright © 2019 by Masjid Uthman (Uthman Academy, Uthman Seminary)

Teachers: Complete and mark all scores and comments up to and including current grade, in pen. **Examiners:** Complete and mark only on top of scores marked by teachers, in thick pen. Add comments in pen.

Comprehensive Assessment (Middle Grades)

Student: _____ Grade: _____ Year: 20____ - 20____

Subject	Grade 4		Grade 5		Grade 6		Grade 7	
	Skill	Score	Skill	Score	Skill	Score	Skill	Score
Quran Reading and Tajwid	Reading Fluency: 15 Quran lines, 3 min		Reading Fluency: 15 Quran lines, 2 min					
	Revise, Identify Tajwid Rules T14-T17a		Revise, Identify Tajwid Rules T14-T17a					
	Reading Fluency: 15 Quran lines, 2.5 min		Reading Fluency: 15 Quran lines, 2 min					
	Revise, Identify Tajwid Rules T17b-T18c		Revise, Identify Tajwid Rules T17b-T18c					
	Reading Fluency: 15 Quran lines, 2 min		Reading Fluency: 15 Quran lines, 2 min					
	Revise, Identify Tajwid Rules T19a-T20e		Revise, Identify Tajwid Rules T19a-T20e					
Quran Memorization	Surah Fajr*		Surah Yasin Ruku 1*		Surah Yasin Ruku 3*			
	Surah Balad*							
	Surah Shams*		Surah Yasin Ruku 2*		Surah Yasin Ruku 4*			
	Surah Layl*							
	Surah Dhuha*							
	Ayat Al-Kursi				Surah Yasin Ruku 5*			
Kalimah and Dua Memorization	Adhan		Protection from Calamities*				Most Comprehensive Dua*	
	Extra Words for Fajr Adhan		At Conclusion of a Gathering		Returning from Journey*		Talbiyah*	
	Reply to Words of Adhan*		When Visiting the Sick*		Protection from Evil Eye		Takbir of Tashriq*	
	After Adhan*		When in Distress*		Sayyidul Istighfar		When Visiting Graveyard	
	Janazah Dua		When Feeling Anger*		When in Market Place*		Time of Burying Deceased*	
	Janazah Dua Male Infant*		Dua at Time of Need (Hajah)		When Having Nightmare		To Benefit from Knowledge*	
	Janazah Dua Female Infant*		Dua on Laylatul Qadr*				At the Time of Death*	
Islamic Studies	Khuff,Masah Wound,Salah Wajib,Sahw,Sawm,Taraw(N4)		Tayam,Salah Sunan,Salah Time,Masbuq,Qada,Id,Hajj(N5)		Water,Impur,Maturl,Imam,Salah Wajib,Janaiz,Jumah (N6)		Salah Makr,Saj,Tilawa,Qasr,Zaka,Inherit,Itikaf,Food(N7)	
	Feeding,Racism,Thank,Friend,Trust,Paradise,Zikr(N4)*		Promises,Tongue,Ghibah,Intox,99Names, Charact (N5)*		Major Sins,Pride,Health,Truth,Love Messeng,Parent (N6)*		Peopleof Jann/Jahan, Ghibah, Modest,Salah Jamah (N7)*	
	Aqaba,Hijra,Treaties,Hypocrit,Badr,Uhud,Ahzab(N4)		Hudaibia,Conquest Makkah,Hunain,Tabuk,Farewell(N5)		Shamail, Abu Bakr (r), Life & Work, Mother Believers (N6)		Shamail, Umar (r), Life and Work (N7)	
	Yaqub (a), Yusuf (a) (N4)		Musa (a), Isa (a) (N5)		Dawud (a), Sulayman (a), Yunus (a), Umayyads (N6)		Zakariyyah (a), Yahya, (a), Abbasids (N7)	
	Mahdi/Dajal/Yajuj/Beast,Trumpet,Qiyama,Bridge(N4)		Death,Janna,Jahanam,Taqdir, Allah/Prophet/Sahaba (N5)		Ahl Sunnah,Prophet,Khulafa,Ash Mubash,Mujiza (N6)		Qada and Qadr, Evil Eye, Life after Death, Barzakh (N7)	
	Trust, Permission Enter, Remov Harm, Neighbor (N4)*		Mashwara, Patience, Kinship, Gifts, Guest, Dhikr (N5)*		Oppression, Bullying, Envy, Ghibah, Pride, Sunnah (N6)*		Spreading Rumors, Value of Time, Knowledge, Durud (N7)*	
	Dua, Dress, Guest/Host, Gathering, Istinja (N4)*		Ghusl, Social Interaction, Writing, Swak, Visit Sick (N5)*		Adhan, Modest Dress, Moderation Expend, Hygiene (N6)*		5 Branches Faith, Oaths, Phone, Elders, Non-Muslims (N7)*	

Adab Akhlaq | Aqaid | Tark Hadi | Sirah | Fiqh

Scoring Key: ✓ Skill acquired prior to this year + Skill acquired this academic year <Blank> Skill not yet acquired or not tested / * Not required for students revising prior grades / **Q** Safar Qaidah Level, **T** Safar Tajwid Level, **N** Nasihah Grade

Examiner Name & Date: _____

Most Recent Comments: _____

Teachers: Complete and mark all scores and comments up to and including current grade, in pen. Examiners: Complete and mark only on top of scores marked by teachers, in thick pen. Add comments in pen.

Copyright © 2019 by Masjid Uthman (Uthman Academy, Uthman Seminary)

Comprehensive Assessment (Elementary Grades)

Student: _____ Grade: _____ Year: 20___ - 20___

Subject	Grade Qaidah		Grade 1		Grade 2		Grade 3	
	Skill	Score	Skill	Score	Skill	Score	Skill	Score
Quran Reading and Tajwid	Pronunciation (alphabet) (Q1)		Ta'wudh, Mim Nun Mushadadah (T14,15)		Ta'wudh, Mim Nun Mushadadah (T14,15)		Reading Fluency: 11 Quran lines, 3 min	
	Letter Recognition (mixed, joined) (Q2)		Qalqalah (T16), Lam of Allah (T17a)		Qalqalah (T16), Lam of Allah (T17a)		Revise, Identify Tajwid Rules T14-T17a	
	Fluency Word, Adv Letter Recog (Q3,4)		Reading Fluency: 5 Quran lines, 3 min		Reading Fluency: 9 Quran lines, 3 min		Reading Fluency: 13 Quran lines, 3 min	
	Harakah (fatha, kasra, dama, tanwin) (Q5)		Ra Mutaharrikah, Sakinah (T17b,c)		Ra Mutaharrikah, Sakinah (T17b,c)		Revise, Identify Tajwid Rules T17b-T18c	
	Stretched Harakahs (stretch, lin) (Q6)		Full-Mouth Letters, Alif (T17d,e)		Full-Mouth Letters, Alif (T17d,e)		Reading Fluency: 15 Quran lines, 3 min	
	Joining Letters (sukun, shad), Madd (Q7,8)		Ikhfa, Idgham, Izhar Shafwi (T18a,b,c)		Ikhfa, Idgham, Izhar Shafwi (T18a,b,c)		Revise, Identify Tajwid Rules T19a-T20e	
	Special Cases, Fluency in 3 Words (Q9,10)		Qalb, Idgham wo/w Ghunnah (T19a,b,c)		Qalb, Idgham wo/w Ghunnah (T19a,b,c)			
	Stopping, Fluency in One Line (Q11,12,13)		Izhar, Ikhfa (T19d,e), Madd (T20a,b,c,d,e)		Izhar, Ikhfa (T19d,e), Madd (T20a,b,c,d,e)			
	All Makharij are Correct		Reading Fluency: 7 Quran lines, 3 min		Reading Fluency: 11 Quran lines, 3 min			
Quran Memorization	Surah Fatihah		Surah Fil		Surah 'Adiyat		Surah Inshirah*	
	Surah Ikhlas		Surah Quraish		Surah Qari'ah		Surah Tin*	
	Surah Falaq		Surah Ma'un		Surah Takathur		Surah Alaq*	
	Surah Nas		Surah Kawthar, Kafirun		Surah Asr		Surah Qadr*	
			Surah Nasr		Surah Humazah		Surah Bayyinah*	
			Surah Lahab				Surah Zilzal*	
Kalimah and Dua Memorization	First Kalimah with Meaning		Takbir Tahrima		Tashahhud		Qunut	
	Second Kalimah with Meaning		Dua Al-Istifta (Thana)				Dua to Make for Parent	
	Ta'awudh, Time Eating, Time Sleeping		Tasbih of Ruku		Durud Ibrahim		Entering a House*	
	Greeting Muslim, Reply to Salam		Rising from Ruku		After Durud Ibrahim		Leaving a House*	
	Drink Water, Hear Messenger (S) Name		In Qawmah		Before Wudu*		When Breaking the Fast	
	We Sneeze, Other Sneezes, Reply Snzng*		Tasbih of Sajdah		After Wudu		When Traveling	
	Entering Washroom, Leaving Washroom*		Between Two Sajdah*		Entering the Masjid		Dua to Make for Host*	
	After Eating, Forget to Recite at Eating		Completing the Salah		Leaving the Masjid*			
	Waking Up							
Islamic Studies			Intro 5 Pillars, Intro Taharah, Wudu Method (N1)		Cleaning Methods,Wudu Detail,Tayam,Salah Method(N2)		NajasTyp,Ghusl,SalaRakt/Cond/Naw,Witr,Musaf,Mard(N3)	
			Feed Hungry, Help, Calmness, Purity, Truth (N1)*		Truth, Salam, Right Hand, Drink, Neighbors (N2)*		Salah,Love,Steadfst,Life,Dua,Guest,Mercy,Shukr(N3)*	
			Childhood,Youth, Marriage Khadijah, Children (N1)		Hira,Revelation,1st Believers,Open Call,Persecut(N2)		Abyssinia,Boycott,Year Sorrow,Taif,Invitation,Miraj(N3)	
			Adam (a), Nuh (a) (N1)		Hud (a), Salih (a) (N2)		Ibrahim (a), Ismail (a), Ishaq (a) (N3)	
			7 Articles, Who is Allah, Provider, Merciful(N1)		Protector,Hearer, Seer, One; Angel; Book; Quran (N2)		Messengers, Qiyamah, Minor Signs, Major Signs (N3)	
			Respect, Cleanliness, Polite, Smile, Right Side (N1)*		Promises,Thanking, Salam, Helping, Animals (N2)*		Thinking Good, Sharing, Parents, Truth, Good Word (N3)*	
			Eat, Drink, Sleeping, Waking, Washroom (N1)*		Greeting, Enter House, Speak, Sneeze, Yawn (N2)*		Traveling, Studying, Quran, Walking, Masjid (N3)*	

Scoring Key: ✓ Skill acquired prior to this year + Skill acquired this academic year <Blank> Skill not yet acquired or not tested / * Not required for students revising prior grades / Q Safar Qaidah Level, T Safar Tajwid Level, N Nasihah Grade

Examiner Name & Date

Comments

Teachers: Complete and mark all scores and comments up to and including current grade, in pen. Examiners: Complete and mark only on top of scores marked by teachers, in thick pen. Add comments in pen.

Copyright © 2019 by Masjid Uthman (Uthman Academy, Uthman Seminary)

Comprehensive Assessment (Middle Grades)

Subject: _____ Student: _____ Grade: _____ Year: 20___ - 20___

Subject		Grade 4		Grade 5		Grade 6		Grade 7	
		Skill	Score	Skill	Score	Skill	Score	Skill	Score
Quran Reading and Tajwid		Reading Fluency: 15 Quran lines, 3 min		Reading Fluency: 15 Quran lines, 2 min					
		Revise, Identify Tajwid Rules T14-T17a		Revise, Identify Tajwid Rules T14-T17a					
		Reading Fluency: 15 Quran lines, 2.5 min		Reading Fluency: 15 Quran lines, 2 min					
		Revise, Identify Tajwid Rules T17b-T18c		Revise, Identify Tajwid Rules T17b-T18c					
		Reading Fluency: 15 Quran lines, 2 min		Reading Fluency: 15 Quran lines, 2 min					
		Revise, Identify Tajwid Rules T19a-T20e		Revise, Identify Tajwid Rules T19a-T20e					
Quran Memorization		Surah Fajr*		Surah Yasin Ruku 1*		Surah Yasin Ruku 3*			
		Surah Balad*							
		Surah Shams*		Surah Yasin Ruku 2*		Surah Yasin Ruku 4*			
		Surah Layl*							
		Surah Dhuha*				Surah Yasin Ruku 5*			
		Ayat Al-Kursi							
Kalimah and Dua Memorization		Adhan		Protection from Calamities*		Returning from Journey*		Most Comprehensive Dua*	
		Extra Words for Fajr Adhan		At Conclusion of a Gathering				Talbiyah*	
		Reply to Words of Adhan*		When Visiting the Sick*		Protection from Evil Eye		Takbir of Tashriq*	
		After Adhan*		When in Distress*		Sayyidul Istighfar		When Visiting Graveyard	
				When Feeling Anger*				Time of Burying Deceased*	
		Janazah Dua		Dua at Time of Need (Hajah)		When in Market Place*		To Benefit from Knowledge*	
		Janazah Dua Male Infant*		Dua on Laylatul Qadr*		When Having Nightmare		At the Time of Death*	
		Janazah Dua Female Infant*							
Islamic Studies	Adab,Akhlaq	Khuff,Masah Wound,Salah Wajib,Sahw,Sawm,Taraw(N4)		Tayam,Salah Sunan,Salah Time,Masbuq,Qada,Id,Hajj(N5)		Water,Impur,Matur,Imam,Salah Wajib,Janaiz,Jumah (N6)		Salah Makr,Saj,Tilawa,Qasr,Zaka,Inherit,Itikaf,Food(N7)	
	Aqaid	Feeding,Racism,Thank,Friend,Trust,Paradise,Zikr(N4)		Promises,Tongue,Ghibah,Intox,99Names,Charact (N5)*		Major Sins,Pride,Health,Truth,Love Messeng,Parent (N6)*		Peopleof Jann/Jahan, Ghibah, Modest, Salah Jamah (N7)*	
	Tark	Aqaba,Hijra,Treaties,Hypocrit,Badr,Uhud,Ahzab(N4)		Hudaibia,Conquest Makkah,Hunain,Tabuk,Farewell (N5)		Shamail,Abu Bakr (r), Life & Work, Mother Believers (N6)		Shamail,Umar (r), Life and Work (N7)	
	Sirah	Yaqub (a), Yusuf (a) (N4)		Musa (a), Isa (a) (N5)		Dawud (a), Sulayman (a), Yunus (a), Umayyads (N6)		Zakariyyah (a), Yahya, (a), Abbasids (N7)	
	Hadi	Mahdi/Dajjal/Yajuj/Beast,Trumpet,Qiyama,Bridge(N4)		Death,Janna,Jahanam,Taqdir, Allah/Prophet/Sahaba (N5)		Ahl Sunnah, Prophet, Khulafa, Ash Mubash, Mujiza (N6)		Qada and Qadr, Evil Eye, Life after Death, Barzakh (N7)	
	Fiqh	Trust, Permission Enter, Remov Harm, Neighbor (N4)*		Mashwara, Patience, Kinship, Gifts, Guest, Dhikr (N5)*		Oppression, Bullying, Envy, Ghibah, Pride, Sunnah (N6)*		Spreading Rumors, Value of Time, Knowledge, Durud (N7)*	
		Dua, Dress, Guest/Host, Gathering, Istinja (N4)*		Ghusl, Social Interaction, Writing, Siwak, Visit Sick (N5)*		Adhan, Modest Dress, Moderation Expend, Hygiene (N6)*		5 Branches Faith, Oaths, Phone, Elders, Non-Muslims (N7)*	

Scoring Key: ✓ Skill acquired prior to this year   + Skill acquired this year   <Blank> Skill not yet acquired or not tested   / * Not required for students revising prior grades   / Q Safar Qaidah Level, T Safar Tajwid Level, N Nasihah Grade

Examiner
Name & Date
Most Recent Comments

Teachers: Complete and mark all scores and comments up to and including current grade, in pen. Examiners: Complete and mark only on top of scores marked by teachers, in thick pen. Add comments in pen.

Copyright © 2019 by Masjid Uthman (Uthman Academy, Uthman Seminary)

Comprehensive Assessment (Elementary Grades)

Grade: _____   Student: _____   Year: 20___ - 20___

Subject	Grade Qaidah Skill	Score	Grade 1 Skill	Score	Grade 2 Skill	Score	Grade 3 Skill	Score
Quran Reading and Tajwid	Pronunciation (alphabet) (Q1)		Ta'wudh, Mim Nun Mushadadah (T14,15)		Ta'wudh, Mim Nun Mushadadah (T14,15)		Reading Fluency: 11 Quran lines, 3 min	
	Letter Recognition (mixed, joined) (Q2)		Qalqalah (T16), Lam of Allah (T17a)		Qalqalah (T16), Lam of Allah (T17a)		Revise, Identify Tajwid Rules T14-T17a	
	Fluency Word, Adv Letter Recog (Q3,4)		Reading Fluency: 5 Quran lines, 3 min		Reading Fluency: 9 Quran lines, 3 min		Reading Fluency: 13 Quran lines, 3 min	
	Harakah (fatha, kasra, dama, tanwin) (Q5)		Ra Mutaharrikah, Sakinah (T17b,c)		Ra Mutaharrikah, Sakinah (T17b,c)		Revise, Identify Tajwid Rules T17b-T18c	
	Stretched Harakahs (stretch, lin) (Q6)		Full-Mouth Letters, Alif (T17d,e)		Full-Mouth Letters, Alif (T17d,e)		Reading Fluency: 15 Quran lines, 3 min	
	Joining Letters (sukun, shad), Madd (Q7,8)		Ikhfa, Idgham, Izhar Shafwi (T18a,b,c)		Ikhfa, Idgham, Izhar Shafwi (T18a,b,c)		Revise, Identify Tajwid Rules T19a-T20e	
	Special Cases, Fluency in 3 Words (Q9,10)		Qalb, Idgham wo/w Ghunnah (T19a,b,c)		Qalb, Idgham wo/w Ghunnah (T19a,b,c)			
	Stopping, Fluency in One Line (Q11,12,13)		Izhar, Ikhfa (T19d,e), Madd (T20a,b,c,d,e)		Izhar, Ikhfa (T19d,e), Madd (T20a,b,c,d,e)			
	All Makharij are Correct		Reading Fluency: 7 Quran lines, 3 min		Reading Fluency: 11 Quran lines, 3 min			
Quran Memorization	Surah Fatihah		Surah Fil		Surah 'Adiyat		Surah Inshirah*	
			Surah Quraish				Surah Tin*	
	Surah Ikhlas		Surah Ma'un		Surah Qari'ah		Surah Alaq*	
	Surah Falaq		Surah Kawthar, Kafirun		Surah Takathur		Surah Qadr*	
	Surah Nas		Surah Nasr		Surah Asr		Surah Bayyinah*	
			Surah Lahab		Surah Humazah		Surah Zilzal*	
Kalimah and Dua Memorization	First Kalimah with Meaning		Takbir Tahrima		Tashahhud		Qunut	
	Second Kalimah with Meaning		Dua Al-Istifta (Thana)				Dua to Make for Parent	
	Ta'awudh, Time Eating, Time Sleeping							
	Greeting Muslim, Reply to Salam		Tasbih of Ruku		Durud Ibrahim		Entering a House*	
	Drink Water, Hear Messenger (S) Name		Rising from Ruku		After Durud Ibrahim		Leaving a House*	
	We Sneeze, Other Sneezes, Reply Snzng*		In Qawmah		Before Wudu*		When Breaking the Fast	
	Entering Washroom, Leaving Washroom*		Tasbih of Sajdah		After Wudu		When Traveling	
	After Eating, Forget to Recite at Eating		Between Two Sajdah*		Entering the Masjid		Dua to Make for Host*	
	Waking Up		Completing the Salah		Leaving the Masjid*			
Islamic Studies			Intro 5 Pillars, Intro Taharah, Wudu Method (N1)		Cleaning Methods,Wudu Detail,Tayam,Salah Method(N2)		Najas Typ,Ghusl,SalaRakt/Cond,Naw,Witr,Musaf,Mard(N3)	
			Feed Hungry, Help,Calmness, Purity, Truth (N1)*		Truth, Salam, Right Hand, Drink, Neighbors (N2)*		Salah,Love,Steadfast,Life,Dua,Guest,Mercy,Shukr(N3)*	
			Childhood,Youth,Marriage Khadijah,Children (N1)		Hira,Revelation,1st Believers,Open Call,Persecut(N2)		Abyssinia,Boycott,Year Sorrow,Taif,Invitation,Miraj(N3)	
			Adam (a), Nuh (a) (N1)		Hud (a), Salih (a) (N2)		Ibrahim (a), Ismail (a), Ishaq (a) (N3)	
			7 Articles, Who is Allah, Provider, Merciful (N1)		Protector,Hearer, Seer, One; Angel; Book; Quran (N2)		Messengers, Qiyamah, Minor Signs, Major Signs (N3)	
			Respect, Cleanliness, Polite, Smile, Right Side (N1)*		Promises,Thanking, Salam, Helping, Animals (N2)*		Thinking Good, Sharing, Parents, Truth, Good Word (N3)*	
			Eat, Drink, Sleeping, Waking, Washroom (N1)*		Greeting, Enter House, Speak, Sneeze, Yawn (N2)*		Traveling, Studying, Quran, Walking, Masjid (N3)*	

Adab/Akhlaq/Aqaid Tarh Sirah/Hadi Fiqh

Scoring Key: ✓ Skill acquired prior to this year / + Skill acquired this academic year / <Blank> Skill not yet acquired or not tested / * Not required for students revising prior grades / Q Safar Qaidah Level, T Safar Tajwid Level, N Nasihah Grade

Examiner Name & Date: _____

Comments: _____

Copyright © 2019 by Masjid Uthman (Uthman Academy, Uthman Seminary)

Teachers: Complete and mark all scores and comments up to and including current grade, in pen. **Examiners:** Complete and mark only on top of scores marked by teachers, in thick pen. Add comments in pen.

Comprehensive Assessment (Middle Grades)

Student: _____ Grade: _____ Year: 20___ - 20___

Subject	Grade 4		Grade 5		Grade 6		Grade 7	
	Skill	Score	Skill	Score	Skill	Score	Skill	Score
Quran Reading and Tajwid	Reading Fluency: 15 Quran lines, 3 min		Reading Fluency: 15 Quran lines, 2 min					
	Revise, Identify Tajwid Rules T14-T17a		Revise, Identify Tajwid Rules T14-T17a					
	Reading Fluency: 15 Quran lines, 2.5 min		Reading Fluency: 15 Quran lines, 2 min					
	Revise, Identify Tajwid Rules T17b-T18c		Revise, Identify Tajwid Rules T17b-T18c					
	Reading Fluency: 15 Quran lines, 2 min		Reading Fluency: 15 Quran lines, 2 min					
	Revise, Identify Tajwid Rules T19a-T20e		Revise, Identify Tajwid Rules T19a-T20e					
Quran Memorization	Surah Fajr*		Surah Yasin Ruku 1*		Surah Yasin Ruku 3*			
	Surah Balad*							
	Surah Shams*		Surah Yasin Ruku 2*		Surah Yasin Ruku 4*			
	Surah Layl*							
	Surah Dhuha*				Surah Yasin Ruku 5*			
	Ayat Al-Kursi							
Kalimah and Dua Memorization	Adhan		Protection from Calamities*		Returning from Journey*		Most Comprehensive Dua*	
	Extra Words for Fajr Adhan		At Conclusion of a Gathering				Talbiyah*	
	Reply to Words of Adhan*		When Visiting the Sick*		Protection from Evil Eye		Takbir of Tashriq*	
	After Adhan*		When in Distress*		Sayyidul Istighfar		When Visiting Graveyard	
	Janazah Dua		When Feeling Anger*		When in Market Place*		Time of Burying Deceased*	
	Janazah Dua Male Infant*		Dua at Time of Need (Hajah)		When Having Nightmare		To Benefit from Knowledge*	
	Janazah Dua Female Infant*		Dua on Laylatul Qadr*				At the Time of Death*	
Islamic Studies	Khuff,Masah Wound,Salah Wajib,Sahw,Sawm,Taraw(N4)		Tayam,Salah Sunan,Salah Time,Masbuq,Qada,I.dHajj(N5)		Water,Impur,Matur,Imam,Salah Wajib,Janaiz,Jumah (N6)		Salah Makr,Saj,Tilawa,Qas,Zaka,Inherit,Itikaf,Food(N7)	
	Feeding,Racism,Thank,Friend,Trust,Paradise,Zikr(N4)		Promises,Tongue,Ghibah,Intox,99Names,Charact (N5)*		Major Sins,Pride,Health,Truth,Love Messeng,Parent (N6)*		People of Jann/Jahan, Ghibah, Modest,Salah Jamah (N7)*	
	Aqaba,Hijra,Treaties,Hypocrit,Badr,Uhud,Ahzab(N4)		Hudaibia,Conquest Makkah,Hunain,Tabuk,Farewell (N5)		Shamail,Abu Bakr (r), Life & Work, Mother Believers (N6)		Shamail,Umar (r), Life and Work (N7)	
	Yaqub (a), Yusuf (a) (N4)		Musa (a), Isa (a) (N5)		Dawud (a), Sulayman (a), Yunus (a), Umayyads (N6)		Zakariyyah (a), Yahya (a), Abbasids (N7)	
	Mahdi/Dajjal/Yajuj/Beast,Trumpet,Qiyama,Bridge(N4)		Death,Janna,Jahanam,Taqdir, Allah/Prophet/Sahaba (N5)		Ahl Sunnah,Prophet,Khulafa,Ash Mubash,Mujiza (N6)		Qada and Qadr, Evil Eye, Life after Death, Barzakh (N7)	
	Trust, Permission Enter, Remov Harm, Neighbor (N4)*		Mashwara, Patience, Kinship, Gifts, Guest, Dhikr (N5)*		Oppression, Bullying, Envy, Ghibah, Pride, Sunnah (N6)*		Spreading Rumors, Value of Time, Knowledge, Durud (N7)*	
	Dua, Dress, Guest/Host, Gathering, Istinja (N4)*		Ghusl, Social Interaction, Writing, Siwak, Visit Sick (N5)*		Adhan, Modest Dress, Moderation Expend, Hygiene (N6)*		5 Branches Faith, Oaths, Phone, Elders, Non-Muslims (N7)*	

(Adab Akhlaq/Aqaid/Tark Hadi Fiqh)

Scoring Key: ✓ Skill acquired prior to this year + Skill acquired this academic year <Blank> Skill not yet acquired or not tested / * Not required for students revising prior grades / Q Safar Qaidah Level, T Safar Tajwid Level, N Nasihah Grade

Examiner

Name & Date

Most Recent Comments

Copyright © 2019 by Masjid Uthman (Uthman Academy, Uthman Seminary)

Teachers: Complete and mark all scores and comments up to and including current grade, in pen. Examiners: Complete and mark only on top of scores marked by teachers, in thick pen. Add comments in pen.

Comprehensive Assessment (Elementary Grades)

Student: _____ Grade: ____ Year: 20___ - 20___

Subject	Grade Qaidah Skill	Score	Grade 1 Skill	Score	Grade 2 Skill	Score	Grade 3 Skill	Score
Quran Reading and Tajwid	Pronunciation (alphabet) (Q1)		Ta'wudh, Mim Nun Mushadadah (T14,15)		Ta'wudh, Mim Nun Mushadadah (T14,15)		Reading Fluency: 11 Quran lines, 3 min	
	Letter Recognition (mixed, joined) (Q2)		Qalqalah (T16), Lam of Allah (T17a)		Qalqalah (T16), Lam of Allah (T17a)		Revise, Identify Tajwid Rules T14-T17a	
	Fluency Word, Adv Letter Recog (Q3,4)		Reading Fluency: 5 Quran lines, 3 min		Reading Fluency: 9 Quran lines, 3 min		Reading Fluency: 13 Quran lines, 3 min	
	Harakah (fatha, kasra, dama, tanwin) (Q5)		Ra Mutaharrikah, Sakinah (T17b,c)		Ra Mutaharrikah, Sakinah (T17b,c)		Revise, Identify Tajwid Rules T17b-T18c	
	Stretched Harakahs (stretch, lin) (Q6)		Full-Mouth Letters, Alif (T17d,e)		Full-Mouth Letters, Alif (T17d,e)		Reading Fluency: 15 Quran lines, 3 min	
	Joining Letters (sukun, shad), Madd (Q7,8)		Ikhfa, Idgham, Izhar Shafwi (T18a,b,c)		Ikhfa, Idgham, Izhar Shafwi (T18a,b,c)		Revise, Identify Tajwid Rules T19a-T20e	
	Special Cases, Fluency in 3 Words (Q9,10)		Qalb, Idgham wo/w Ghunnah (T19a,b,c)		Qalb, Idgham wo/w Ghunnah (T19a,b,c)			
	Stopping, Fluency in One Line (Q11,12,13)		Izhar, Ikhfa (T19d,e), Madd (T20a,b,c,d,e)		Izhar, Ikhfa (T19d,e), Madd (T20a,b,c,d,e)			
	All Makharij are Correct		Reading Fluency: 7 Quran lines, 3 min		Reading Fluency: 11 Quran lines, 3 min			
Quran Memorization	Surah Fatihah		Surah Fil		Surah 'Adiyat		Surah Inshirah*	
			Surah Quraish				Surah Tin*	
	Surah Ikhlas		Surah Ma'un		Surah Qari'ah		Surah Alaq*	
	Surah Falaq		Surah Kawthar, Kafirun		Surah Takathur		Surah Qadr*	
	Surah Nas		Surah Nasr		Surah Asr		Surah Bayyinah*	
			Surah Lahab		Surah Humazah		Surah Zilzal*	
Kalimah and Dua Memorization	First Kalimah with Meaning		Takbir Tahrima		Tashahhud		Qunut	
	Second Kalimah with Meaning		Dua Al-Istifta (Thana)				Dua to Make for Parent	
	Ta'awudh, Time Eating, Time Sleeping							
	Greeting Muslim, Reply to Salam		Tasbih of Ruku		Durud Ibrahim		Entering a House*	
	Drink Water, Hear Messenger (S) Name		Rising from Ruku		After Durud Ibrahim		Leaving a House*	
	We Sneeze, Other Sneezes, Reply Snzng*		In Qawmah		Before Wudu*		When Breaking the Fast	
	Entering Washroom, Leaving Washroom*		Tasbih of Sajdah		After Wudu		When Traveling	
	After Eating, Forget to Recite at Eating		Between Two Sajdah*		Entering the Masjid		Dua to Make for Host*	
	Waking Up		Completing the Salah		Leaving the Masjid*			
Islamic Studies			Intro 5 Pillars, Intro Taharah, Wudu Method (N1)		Cleaning Methods,Wudu Detail,Tayam,Salah Method(N2)		Najas,Typ,Ghusl,SalaRakt/Cond/Naw,Witr,Musaf,Mard(N3)	
			Feed Hungry, Help, Calmness, Purity, Truth (N1)*		Truth, Salam, Right Hand, Drink, Neighbors (N2)*		Salah,Love,Steadfst,Life,Dua,Guest,Mercy,Shukr(N3)*	
			Childhood, Youth, Marriage Khadijah, Children (N1)		Hira,Revelation,1st Believers,Open Call,Persecut(N2)		Abyssinia,Boycott,Year Sorrow,Taif,Invitation,Miraj(N3)	
			Adam (a), Nuh (a) (N1)		Hud (a), Salih (a) (N2)		Ibrahim (a), Ismail (a), Ishaq (a) (N3)	
			7 Articles, Who is Allah, Provider, Merciful (N1)		Protector, Hearer, Seer, One; Angel; Book; Quran (N2)		Messengers, Qiyamah, Minor Signs, Major Signs (N3)	
			Respect, Cleanliness, Polite, Smile, Right Side (N1)*		Promises,Thanking, Salam, Helping, Animals (N2)*		Thinking Good, Sharing, Parents, Truth, Good Word (N3)*	
			Eat, Drink, Sleeping, Waking, Washroom (N1)*		Greeting, Enter House, Speak, Sneeze, Yawn (N2)*		Traveling, Studying, Quran, Walking, Masjid (N3)*	

Scoring Key: ✓ Skill acquired prior to this year / + Skill acquired this academic year / <Blank> Skill not yet acquired or not tested / * Not required for students revising prior grades / Q Safar Qaidah Level, T Safar Tajwid Level, N Nasihah Grade

Examiner Name & Date: _____

Comments: _____

Copyright © 2019 by Masjid Uthman (Uthman Academy, Uthman Seminary)

Teachers: Complete and mark all scores and comments up to and including current grade, in pen. Examiners: Complete and mark only on top of scores marked by teachers, in thick pen. Add comments in pen.

Comprehensive Assessment (Middle Grades)

Student: _____ Grade: _____ Year: 20____ - 20____

Subject		Grade 4		Grade 5		Grade 6		Grade 7	
		Skill	Score	Skill	Score	Skill	Score	Skill	Score
Quran Reading and Tajwid		Reading Fluency: 15 Quran lines, 3 min		Reading Fluency: 15 Quran lines, 2 min					
		Revise, Identify Tajwid Rules T14-T17a		Revise, Identify Tajwid Rules T14-T17a					
		Reading Fluency: 15 Quran lines, 2.5 min		Reading Fluency: 15 Quran lines, 2 min					
		Revise, Identify Tajwid Rules T17b-T18c		Revise, Identify Tajwid Rules T17b-T18c					
		Reading Fluency: 15 Quran lines, 2 min		Reading Fluency: 15 Quran lines, 2 min					
		Revise, Identify Tajwid Rules T19a-T20e		Revise, Identify Tajwid Rules T19a-T20e					
Quran Memorization		Surah Fajr*		Surah Yasin Ruku 1*		Surah Yasin Ruku 3*			
		Surah Balad*							
		Surah Shams*							
		Surah Layl*		Surah Yasin Ruku 2*		Surah Yasin Ruku 4*			
		Surah Dhuha*							
		Ayat Al-Kursi				Surah Yasin Ruku 5*			
Kalimah and Dua Memorization		Adhan		Protection from Calamities*				Most Comprehensive Dua*	
		Extra Words for Fajr Adhan		At Conclusion of a Gathering		Returning from Journey*		Talbiyah*	
		Reply to Words of Adhan*		When Visiting the Sick*		Protection from Evil Eye		Takbir of Tashriq*	
		After Adhan*		When in Distress*		Sayyidul Istighfar		When Visiting Graveyard	
		Janazah Dua		When Feeling Anger*		When in Market Place*		Time of Burying Deceased*	
		Janazah Dua Male Infant*		Dua at Time of Need (Hajah)		When Having Nightmare		To Benefit from Knowledge*	
		Janazah Dua Female Infant*		Dua on Laylatul Qadr*				At the Time of Death*	
Islamic Studies	Adab,Akhlaq,Aqaid,Tark,Sirah,Hadi,Fiqh	Khuff,Masah,Wound,Salah Wajib,Sahw,Sawm,Taraw(N4)		Tayam,Salah Sunan,Salah Time,Masbuq,Qada,Id,Hajj(N5)		Water,Impur,Matur,Imam,Salah Wajib,Janaiz,Jumah (N6)		Salah Makr,Saj,Tilawa,Qasr,Zaka,Inherit,Itikaf,Food(N7)	
		Feeding,Racism,Thank,Friend,Trust,Paradise,Zikr(N4)*		Promises,Tongue,Ghibah,Intox,99Names,Charact (N5)*		Major Sins,Pride,Health,Truth,Love Messeng,Parent (N6)*		People of Jann/Jahan, Ghibah, Modest,Salah Jamah (N7)	
		Aqaba,Hijra,Treaties,Hypocrit,Badr,Uhud,Ahzab(N4)		Hudaibia,Conquest Makkah,Hunain,Tabuk,Farewell (N5)		Shamail, Abu Bakr (r), Life & Work, Mother Believers (N6)		Shamail, Umar (r), Life and Work (N7)	
		Yaqub (a), Yusuf (a) (N4)		Musa (a), Isa (a) (N5)		Dawud (a), Sulayman (a), Yunus (a), Umayyads (N6)		Zakariyyah (a), Yahya, (a), Abbasids (N7)	
		Mahdi/Dajal/Yajuj/Beast,Trumpet,Qiyama,Bridge(N4)		Death,Janna,Jahanam,Taqdir, Allah/Prophet/Sahaba (N5)		Ahl Sunnah,Prophet,Khulafa,Ash Mubash,Mujiza (N6)		Qada and Qadr, Evil Eye, Life after Death, Barzakh (N7)	
		Trust, Permission Enter, Remov Harm, Neighbor (N4)*		Mashwara, Patience, Kinship, Gifts, Guest, Dhikr (N5)*		Oppression, Bullying, Envy, Ghibah, Pride, Sunnah (N6)*		Spreading Rumors, Value of Time, Knowledge, Durud (N7)*	
		Dua, Dress, Guest/Host, Gathering, Istinja (N4)*		Ghusl, Social Interaction, Writing, Siwak, Visit Sick (N5)*		Adhan, Modest Dress, Moderation Expend, Hygiene (N6)*		5 Branches Faith, Oaths, Phone, Elders, Non-Muslims (N7)*	

Scoring Key: ✓ Skill acquired prior to this year + Skill acquired this academic year <Blank> Skill not yet acquired or not tested / *Not required for students revising prior grades / Q Safar Qaidah Level, T Safar Tajwid Level, N Nasihah Grade

Examiner	
Name & Date	
Most Recent Comments	

Teachers: Complete and mark all scores and comments up to and including current grade, in pen. Examiners: Complete and mark only on top of scores marked by teachers, in thick pen. Add comments in pen.

Copyright © 2019 by Masjid Uthman (Uthman Academy, Uthman Seminary)

Comprehensive Assessment (Elementary Grades)

Student: _____ Grade: _____ Year: 20___ - 20___

Subject	Grade Qaidah		Grade 1		Grade 2		Grade 3	
	Skill	Score	Skill	Score	Skill	Score	Skill	Score
Quran Reading and Tajwid	Pronunciation (alphabet) (Q1)		Ta'wudh, Mim Nun Mushadadah (T14,15)		Ta'wudh, Mim Nun Mushadadah (T14,15)		Reading Fluency: 11 Quran lines, 3 min	
	Letter Recognition (mixed, joined) (Q2)		Qalqalah (T16), Lam of Allah (T17a)		Qalqalah (T16), Lam of Allah (T17a)		Revise, Identify Tajwid Rules T14-T17a	
	Fluency Word, Adv Letter Recog (Q3,4)		Reading Fluency: 5 Quran lines, 3 min		Reading Fluency: 9 Quran lines, 3 min		Reading Fluency: 13 Quran lines, 3 min	
	Harakah (fatha, kasra, dama, tanwin) (Q5)		Ra Mutaharrikah, Sakinah (T17b,c)		Ra Mutaharrikah, Sakinah (T17b,c)		Revise, Identify Tajwid Rules T17b-T18c	
	Stretched Harakahs (stretch, lin) (Q6)		Full-Mouth Letters, Alif (T17d,e)		Full-Mouth Letters, Alif (T17d,e)		Reading Fluency: 15 Quran lines, 3 min	
	Joining Letters (sukun, shad), Madd (Q7,8)		Ikhfa, Idgham, Izhar Shafwi (T18a,b,c)		Ikhfa, Idgham, Izhar Shafwi (T18a,b,c)		Revise, Identify Tajwid Rules T19a-T20e	
	Special Cases, Fluency in 3 Words (Q9,10)		Qalb, Idgham w/o w Ghunnah (T19a,b,c)		Qalb, Idgham w/o w Ghunnah (T19a,b,c)			
	Stopping, Fluency in One Line (Q11,12,13)		Izhar, Ikhfa (T19d,e), Madd (T20a,b,c,d,e)		Izhar, Ikhfa (T19d,e), Madd (T20a,b,c,d,e)			
	All Makharij are Correct		Reading Fluency: 7 Quran lines, 3 min		Reading Fluency: 11 Quran lines, 3 min			
Quran Memorization	Surah Fatihah		Surah Fil		Surah 'Adiyat		Surah Inshirah*	
			Surah Quraish				Surah Tin*	
	Surah Ikhlas		Surah Ma'un		Surah Qari'ah		Surah Alaq*	
	Surah Falaq		Surah Kawthar, Kafirun		Surah Takathur		Surah Qadr*	
			Surah Nasr		Surah Asr		Surah Bayyinah*	
	Surah Nas		Surah Lahab		Surah Humazah		Surah Zilzal*	
Kalimah and Dua Memorization	First Kalimah with Meaning		Takbir Tahrima		Tashahhud		Qunut	
	Second Kalimah with Meaning		Dua Al-Istifta (Thana)				Dua to Make for Parent	
	Ta'awudh, Time Eating, Time Sleeping							
	Greeting Muslim, Reply to Salam		Tasbih of Ruku		Durud Ibrahim		Entering a House*	
	Drink Water, Hear Messenger (S) Name		Rising from Ruku		After Durud Ibrahim		Leaving a House*	
	We Sneeze, Other Sneezes, Reply Snzng*		In Qawmah		Before Wudu*		When Breaking the Fast	
	Entering Washroom, Leaving Washroom*		Tasbih of Sajdah		After Wudu		When Traveling	
	After Eating, Forget to Recite at Eating		Between Two Sajdah*		Entering the Masjid		Dua to Make for Host*	
	Waking Up		Completing the Salah		Leaving the Masjid*			
Islamic Studies			Intro 5 Pillars, Intro Taharah, Wudu Method (N1)		Cleaning Methods,Wudu Detail,Tayam,Salah Method(N2)		Najas,Typ,Ghus,SalaRakt/Cond/Naw,Witr,Musaf,Mard(N3)	
			Feed Hungry, Help, Calmness, Purity, Truth (N1)*		Truth, Salam, Right Hand, Drink, Neighbors (N2)*		Salah,Love,Steadfst,Life,Dua,Guest,Mercy,Shukr(N3)*	
			Childhood,Youth, Marriage Khadijah, Children (N1)		Hira,Revelation,1st Believers,Open Call,Persecut(N2)		Abyssinia,Boycott,Year Sorrow,Taif,Invitation,Miraj(N3)	
			Adam (a), Nuh (a) (N1)		Hud (a), Salih (a) (N2)		Ibrahim (a), Ismail (a), Ishaq (a) (N3)	
			7 Articles, Who is Allah, Provider, Merciful (N1)		Protector, Hearer, Seer, One; Angel; Book; Quran (N2)		Messengers, Qiyamah, Minor Signs, Major Signs (N3)	
			Respect, Cleanliness, Polite, Smile, Right Side (N1)*		Promises, Thanking, Salam, Helping, Animals (N2)*		Thinking Good, Sharing, Parents, Truth, Good Word (N3)*	
			Eat, Drink, Sleeping, Waking, Washroom (N1)*		Greeting, Enter House, Speak, Sneeze, Yawn (N2)*		Traveling, Studying, Quran, Walking, Masjid (N3)*	

Scoring Key: ✓ Skill acquired prior to this year + Skill acquired this academic year <Blank> Skill not yet acquired or not tested / * Not required for students revising prior grades / Q Safar Qaidah Level, T Safar Tajwid Level, N Nasihah Grade

Adab/Akhlaq/Aqaid/Tark Sirah/Hadi Fiqh

Examiner Name & Date		
Comments		

Teachers: Complete and mark all scores and comments up to and including current grade, in pen. Examiners: Complete and mark only on top of scores marked by teachers, in thick pen. Add comments in pen.

Copyright © 2019 by Masjid Uthman (Uthman Academy, Uthman Seminary)

Comprehensive Assessment (Middle Grades)

Subject: _____ Student: _____ Grade: _____ Year: 20___ - 20___

Subject	Grade 4 Skill	Score	Grade 5 Skill	Score	Grade 6 Skill	Score	Grade 7 Skill	Score
Quran Reading and Tajwid	Reading Fluency: 15 Quran lines, 3 min		Reading Fluency: 15 Quran lines, 2 min					
	Revise, Identify Tajwid Rules T14-T17a		Revise, Identify Tajwid Rules T14-T17a					
	Reading Fluency: 15 Quran lines, 2.5 min		Reading Fluency: 15 Quran lines, 2 min					
	Revise, Identify Tajwid Rules T17b-T18c		Revise, Identify Tajwid Rules T17b-T18c					
	Reading Fluency: 15 Quran lines, 2 min		Reading Fluency: 15 Quran lines, 2 min					
	Revise, Identify Tajwid Rules T19a-T20e		Revise, Identify Tajwid Rules T19a-T20e					
Quran Memorization	Surah Fajr*		Surah Balad*		Surah Yasin Ruku 3*			
	Surah Shams*		Surah Layl*		Surah Yasin Ruku 4*			
	Surah Dhuha*		Ayat Al-Kursi		Surah Yasin Ruku 5*			
			Surah Yasin Ruku 1*					
			Surah Yasin Ruku 2*					
Kalimah and Dua Memorization	Adhan		Protection from Calamities*		Returning from Journey*		Most Comprehensive Dua*	
	Extra Words for Fajr Adhan		At Conclusion of a Gathering		Protection from Evil Eye		Talbiyah*	
	Reply to Words of Adhan*		When Visiting the Sick*		Sayyidul Istighfar		Takbir of Tashriq*	
	After Adhan*		When in Distress*		When in Market Place*		When Visiting Graveyard	
	Janazah Dua		When Feeling Anger*		When Having Nightmare		Time of Burying Deceased*	
	Janazah Dua Male Infant*		Dua at Time of Need (Hajah)				To Benefit from Knowledge*	
	Janazah Dua Female Infant*		Dua on Laylatul Qadr*				At the Time of Death*	
Islamic Studies	Khuff,Masah Wound,Salah Wajib,Sahw,Sawm,Tarawi(N4)		Tayam,Salah Sunan,Salah Time,Masbuq,Qada,i.d.Hajj (N5)		Water,i,mpur,Matur,imam,Salah Wajib,Janaiz,Jumah (N6)		Salah Makr,Saj,Tilawa,Qasr,Zaka,I.nherit,Itikaf,Food (N7)	
	Feeding,Racism,Thank,Friend,Trust,Paradise,2ikr (N4)*		Promises,Tongue,Ghibah,Intox,99Names,Charact (N5)*		Major Sins,Pride,Health,Truth,Love Messeng,Parent (N6)*		People of Jann/Jahan, Ghibah, Modest, Salah Jamah (N7)*	
	Aqaba,Hijra,Treaties,Hypocrit,Badri,Uhud,Ahzab (N4)		Hudaibia,Conquest Makkah,Hunain,Tabuk,Farewell (N5)		Shamail,Abu Bakr (r.), Life & Work, Mother Believers (N6)		Shamail, Umar (r.), Life and Work (N7)	
	Yaqub (a), Yusuf (a) (N4)		Musa (a), Isa (a) (N5)		Dawud (a), Sulayman (a), Yunus (a), Umayyads (N6)		Zakariyyah (a), Yahya (a), Abbasids (N7)	
	Mahdi/Dajjal/Yajuj/Beast,Trumpet,Qiyama,Bridge (N4)		Death,Janna,Jahanam,Taqdir, Allah/Prophet/Sahaba (N5)		Ahl Sunnah,Prophet,Khulafa,Ash Mubash,Mujiza (N6)		Qada and Qadr, Evil Eye, Life after Death, Barzakh (N7)	
	Trust, Permission Enter, Remov Harm, Neighbor (N4)*		Mashwara, Patience, Kinship, Gifts, Guest, Dhikr (N5)*		Oppression, Bullying, Envy, Ghibah, Pride, Sunnah (N6)*		Spreading Rumors, Value of Time, Knowledge, Durud (N7)*	
	Dua,Dress,Guest/Host,Gathering,Istinja (N4)*		Ghusl, Social interaction, Writing, Siwak, Visit Sick (N5)*		Adhan, Modest Dress, Moderation Expend, Hygiene (N6)*		5 Branches Faith, Oaths, Phone, Elders, Non-Muslims (N7)*	

Adab Akhlaq / Aqaid / Tarikh / Sirah / Hadi / Fiqh

Scoring Key: ✓ Skill acquired prior to this year + Skill acquired this academic year <Blank> Skill not yet acquired or not tested / * Not required for students revising prior grades / **Q** Safar Qaidah Level, **T** Safar Tajwid Level, **N** Nasihah Grade

Examiner
Name & Date

Most Recent Comments

Copyright © 2019 by Masjid Uthman (Uthman Academy, Uthman Seminary)

Teachers: Complete and mark all scores and comments up to and including current grade, in pen. **Examiners:** Complete and mark only on top of scores marked by teachers, in thick pen. Add comments in pen.

Comprehensive Assessment (Elementary Grades)

Student: _____ Grade: _____ Year: 20___ - 20___

Subject	Grade Qaidah Skill	Score	Grade 1 Skill	Score	Grade 2 Skill	Score	Grade 3 Skill	Score
Quran Reading and Tajwid	Pronunciation (alphabet) (Q1)		Ta'wudh, Mim Nun Mushadadah (T14,15)		Ta'wudh, Mim Nun Mushadadah (T14,15)		Reading Fluency: 11 Quran lines, 3 min	
	Letter Recognition (mixed, joined) (Q2)		Qalqalah (T16), Lam of Allah (T17a)		Qalqalah (T16), Lam of Allah (T17a)		Revise, Identify Tajwid Rules T14-T17a	
	Fluency Word, Adv Letter Recog (Q3,4)		Reading Fluency: 5 Quran lines, 3 min		Reading Fluency: 9 Quran lines, 3 min		Reading Fluency: 13 Quran lines, 3 min	
	Harakah (fatha, kasra, dama, tanwin) (Q5)		Ra Mutaharrikah, Sakinah (T17b,c)		Ra Mutaharrikah, Sakinah (T17b,c)		Revise, Identify Tajwid Rules T17b-T18c	
	Stretched Harakahs (stretch, lin) (Q6)		Full-Mouth Letters, Alif (T17d,e)		Full-Mouth Letters, Alif (T17d,e)		Reading Fluency: 15 Quran lines, 3 min	
	Joining Letters (sukun, shad), Madd (Q7,8)		Ikhfa, Idgham, Izhar Shafwi (T18a,b,c)		Ikhfa, Idgham, Izhar Shafwi (T18a,b,c)		Revise, Identify Tajwid Rules T19a-T20e	
	Special Cases, Fluency in 3 Words (Q9,10)		Qalb, Idgham wo/w Ghunnah (T19a,b,c)		Qalb, Idgham wo/w Ghunnah (T19a,b,c)			
	Stopping, Fluency in One Line (Q11,12,13)		Izhar, Ikhfa (T19d,e), Madd (T20a,b,c,d,e)		Izhar, Ikhfa (T19d,e), Madd (T20a,b,c,d,e)			
	All Makharij are Correct		Reading Fluency: 7 Quran lines, 3 min		Reading Fluency: 11 Quran lines, 3 min			
Quran Memorization	Surah Fatihah		Surah Fil		Surah 'Adiyat		Surah Inshirah*	
	Surah Ikhlas		Surah Quraish				Surah Tin*	
	Surah Falaq		Surah Ma'un		Surah Qari'ah		Surah Alaq*	
	Surah Nas		Surah Kawthar, Kafirun		Surah Takathur		Surah Qadr*	
			Surah Nasr		Surah Asr		Surah Bayyinah*	
			Surah Lahab		Surah Humazah		Surah Zilzal*	
Kalimah and Dua Memorization	First Kalimah with Meaning		Takbir Tahrima		Tashahhud		Qunut	
	Second Kalimah with Meaning		Dua Al-Istifta (Thana)				Dua to Make for Parent	
	Ta'awudh, Time Eating, Time Sleeping							
	Greeting Muslim, Reply to Salam		Tasbih of Ruku		Durud Ibrahim		Entering a House*	
	Drink Water, Hear Messenger (S) Name		Rising from Ruku		After Durud Ibrahim		Leaving a House*	
	We Sneeze, Other Sneezes, Reply Snzng*		In Qawmah		Before Wudu*		When Breaking the Fast	
	Entering Washroom, Leaving Washroom*		Tasbih of Sajdah		After Wudu		When Traveling	
	After Eating, Forget to Recite at Eating		Between Two Sajdah*		Entering the Masjid		Dua to Make for Host*	
	Waking Up		Completing the Salah		Leaving the Masjid*			
Islamic Studies			Intro 5 Pillars, Intro Taharah, Wudu Method (N1)		Cleaning Methods,Wudu Detail,Tayam,Salah Method(N2)		Najas,Typ,Ghusl,SaaRakt/Cond/Naw,Witr,Musaf,Mard(N3)	
			Feed Hungry, Help,Calmness, Purity, Truth (N1)*		Truth, Salam, Right Hand, Drink, Neighbors (N2)*		Salah,Love,Steadfst,Life,Dua,Guest,Mercy,Shukr(N3)*	
			Childhood, Youth, Marriage Khadijah, Children (N1)		Hira,Revelation,1st Believers,Open Call,Persecut(N2)		Abyssinia,Boycott,Year Sorrow,Taif,Invitation,Miraj(N3)	
			Adam (a), Nuh (a) (N1)		Hud (a), Salih (a) (N2)		Ibrahim (a), Ismail (a), Ishaq (a) (N3)	
			7 Articles, Who is Allah, Provider, Merciful (N1)		Protector, Hearer, Seer, One; Angel; Book; Quran (N2)		Messengers, Qiyamah, Minor Signs, Major Signs (N3)	
			Respect, Cleanliness, Polite, Smile, Right Side (N1)*		Promises, Thanking, Salam, Helping, Animals (N2)*		Thinking Good,Sharing,Parents,Truth, Good Word (N3)*	
			Eat, Drink, Sleeping, Waking, Washroom (N1)*		Greeting, Enter House, Speak, Sneeze, Yawn (N2)*		Traveling, Studying, Quran, Walking, Masjid (N3)*	

Side label: Adab/Akhlaq, Aqaid, Tarikh, Hadith, Fiqh

Scoring Key: ✓ Skill acquired prior to this year + Skill acquired this academic year <Blank> Skill not yet acquired or not tested / * Not required for students revising prior grades / Q Safar Qaidah Level, T Safar Tajwid Level, N Nasihah Grade

Examiner Name & Date: _____

Comments: _____

Teachers: Complete and mark all scores and comments up to and including current grade, in pen. Examiners: Complete and mark only on top of scores marked by teachers, in thick pen. Add comments in pen.

Copyright © 2019 by Masjid Uthman (Uthman Academy, Uthman Seminary)

Comprehensive Assessment (Middle Grades)

Student: _____ Grade: _____ Year: 20___ - 20___

Subject	Grade 4		Grade 5		Grade 6		Grade 7	
	Skill	Score	Skill	Score	Skill	Score	Skill	Score
Quran Reading and Tajwid	Reading Fluency: 15 Quran lines, 3 min		Reading Fluency: 15 Quran lines, 2 min					
	Revise, Identify Tajwid Rules T14-T17a		Revise, Identify Tajwid Rules T14-T17a					
	Reading Fluency: 15 Quran lines, 2.5 min		Reading Fluency: 15 Quran lines, 2 min					
	Revise, Identify Tajwid Rules T17b-T18c		Revise, Identify Tajwid Rules T17b-T18c					
	Reading Fluency: 15 Quran lines, 2 min		Reading Fluency: 15 Quran lines, 2 min					
	Revise, Identify Tajwid Rules T19a-T20e		Revise, Identify Tajwid Rules T19a-T20e					
Quran Memorization	Surah Fajr*		Surah Yasin Ruku 1*		Surah Yasin Ruku 3*			
	Surah Balad*							
	Surah Shams*							
	Surah Layl*		Surah Yasin Ruku 2*		Surah Yasin Ruku 4*			
	Surah Dhuha*							
	Ayat Al-Kursi				Surah Yasin Ruku 5*			
Kalimah and Dua Memorization	Adhan		Protection from Calamities*				Most Comprehensive Dua*	
	Extra Words for Fajr Adhan		At Conclusion of a Gathering		Returning from Journey*		Talbiyah*	
	Reply to Words of Adhan*		When Visiting the Sick*		Protection from Evil Eye		Takbir of Tashriq*	
	After Adhan*		When in Distress*		Sayyidul Istighfar		When Visiting Graveyard	
	Janazah Dua		When Feeling Anger*		When in Market Place*		Time of Burying Deceased*	
	Janazah Dua Male Infant*		Dua at Time of Need (Hajah)		When Having Nightmare		To Benefit from Knowledge*	
	Janazah Dua Female Infant*		Dua on Laylatul Qadr*				At the Time of Death*	
Islamic Studies (Adab, Akhlaq, Aqaid, Tark, Sirah, Hadi, Fiqh)	Khuff, Masah Wound, Salah Wajib, Sahw, Sawm, Taraw (N4)		Tayam, Salah Sunan, Salah Time, Masbuq, Qada, Id, Haji (N5)		Water, Impur, Matur, Imam Salah Wajib, Janaiz, Jumah (N6)		Salah Makr, Saj, Tilawa, Qasr, Zaka, Inherit, Itikaf, Food (N7)	
	Feeding, Racism, Thank, Friend, Trust, Paradise, Zikr (N4)*		Promises, Tongue, Ghibah, Intox, 99Names, Charact (N5)*		Major Sins, Pride, Health, Truth, Love Messeng, Parent (N6)*		Peopleof Jann/Jahan, Ghibah, Modest, Salah Jamah (N7)*	
	Aqaba, Hijra, Treaties, Hypocrit, Badr, Uhud, Ahzab (N4)		Hudaibia, Conquest Makkah, Hunain, Tabuk, Farewell (N5)		Shamail, Abu Bakr (r), Life & Work, Mother Believers (N6)		Shamail, Umar (r), Life and Work (N7)	
	Yaqub (a), Yusuf (a) (N4)		Musa (a), Isa (a) (N5)		Dawud (a), Sulayman (a), Yunus (a), Umayyads (N6)		Zakariyyah (a), Yahya, (a), Abbasids (N7)	
	Mahdi/Dajjal/Yajuj/Beast, Trumpet, Qiyama, Bridge (N4)		Death, Janna, Jahanam, Taqdir, Allah/Prophet/Sahaba (N5)		Ahl Sunnah, Prophet, Khulafa, Ash Mubash, Mujiza (N6)		Qada and Qadr, Evil Eye, Life after Death, Barzaakh (N7)	
	Trust, Permission Enter, Remov Harm, Neighbor (N4)*		Mashwara, Patience, Kinship, Gifts, Guest, Dhikr (N5)*		Oppression, Bullying, Envy, Ghibah, Pride, Sunnah (N6)*		Spreading Rumors, Value of Time, Knowledge, Durud (N7)*	
	Dua, Dress, Guest/Host, Gathering, Istinja (N4)*		Ghusl, Social Interaction, Writing, Siwak, Visit Sick (N5)*		Adhan, Modest Dress, Moderation Expend, Hygiene (N6)*		5 Branches Faith, Oaths, Phone, Elders, Non-Muslims (N7)*	

Scoring Key: ✓ Skill acquired prior to this year + Skill acquired this academic year <Blank> Skill not yet acquired or not tested / * Not required for students revising prior grades / **Q** Safar Qaidah Level, **T** Safar Tajwid Level, **N** Nasihah Grade

Examiner	
Name & Date	
Most Recent Comments	

Teachers: Complete and mark all scores and comments up to and including current grade, in pen. Examiners: Complete and mark only on top of scores marked by teachers, in thick pen. Add comments in pen.

Copyright © 2019 by Masjid Uthman (Uthman Academy, Uthman Seminary)

Masjid Uthman

After School Islamic & Quran Studies
Trimester 1 Report Card

Student Name: _____   Grade: _____

Subject	Grade	Comments
Quran Reading and Tajwid		❑ Qaidah ❑ Nazirah (Reading): Fluency: _____ lines / 3 min
Covered this trimester:		
Quran Memorization		
Covered this trimester:		
Kalimah and Dua Memorization		
Covered this trimester:		
Islamic Studies		
❑ Fiqh ❑ Ahadith ❑ Sirah ❑ Tarikh ❑ Aqaid ❑ Akhlaq ❑ Adab		
Covered this trimester:		
❑ Fiqh ❑ Ahadith ❑ Sirah ❑ Tarikh ❑ Aqaid ❑ Akhlaq ❑ Adab		
Covered this trimester:		

_____   _____
Teacher   Date

A Excellent (90-100%), **B** Good (80-89%), **C** Fair (70-79%), **D** Poor (60-69%), **F** Failing, **NA** Not Applicable

Masjid Uthman

After School Islamic & Quran Studies
Trimester 2 Report Card

Student Name: _____   Grade: _____

Subject	Grade	Comments
Quran Reading and Tajwid		❑ Qaidah ❑ Nazirah (Reading): Fluency: ____ lines / 3 min
Covered this trimester:		
Quran Memorization		
Covered this trimester:		
Kalimah and Dua Memorization		
Covered this trimester:		
Islamic Studies		
❑ Fiqh ❑ Ahadith ❑ Sirah ❑ Tarikh ❑ Aqaid ❑ Akhlaq ❑ Adab		
Covered this trimester:		
❑ Fiqh ❑ Ahadith ❑ Sirah ❑ Tarikh ❑ Aqaid ❑ Akhlaq ❑ Adab		
Covered this trimester:		

_____   _____
Teacher   Date

A Excellent (90-100%), **B** Good (80-89%), **C** Fair (70-79%), **D** Poor (60-69%), **F** Failing, **NA** Not Applicable

Masjid Uthman

After School Islamic & Quran Studies
Trimester 3 Report Card

Student Name: _____   Grade: _____

Subject	Grade	Comments
Quran Reading and Tajwid		❏ Qaidah ❏ Nazirah (Reading): Fluency: ____ lines / 3 min
Covered this trimester:		
Quran Memorization		
Covered this trimester:		
Kalimah and Dua Memorization		
Covered this trimester:		
Islamic Studies		
❏ Fiqh ❏ Ahadith ❏ Sirah ❏ Tarikh ❏ Aqaid ❏ Akhlaq ❏ Adab		
Covered this trimester:		
❏ Fiqh ❏ Ahadith ❏ Sirah ❏ Tarikh ❏ Aqaid ❏ Akhlaq ❏ Adab		
Covered this trimester:		

_____   _____
Teacher   Date

A Excellent (90-100%), **B** Good (80-89%), **C** Fair (70-79%), **D** Poor (60-69%), **F** Failing, **NA** Not Applicable

After School Islamic and Quran Studies Curriculum

Subject	Grade Qaidah (Ages 5-6)	Grade 1 (Ages 6-7)	Grade 2 (Ages 7-8)
Quran Reading	Group 1 • Safar Qaidah (start at the very beginning and complete book) Group 2 (students who at beginning of year recognize advanced joined letters at Safar Qaidah Level 4.) • Safar Qaidah (start at Q5a and complete book) • Quran Recitation (Juz 1 partial) *Quran Reading subject is 60-70 min. Remaining subjects are 10-20 min.*	• Safar Rules of Tajwid (complete) • Quran Recitation (Juz 1-2) *Quran Reading subject is 55-60 min. Remaining subjects are 20-30 min.*	• Safar Rules of Tajwid (complete) • Quran Recitation (Juz 3-5) *Quran Reading subject is 55-60 min. Remaining subjects are 20-30 min.*
Quran Memorization	New Memorization • Surah Fatihah • Surah Ikhlas • Surah Falaq • Surah Nas	Revision • Old students revise all surahs from Grade Qaidah • New students memorize all surahs from Grade Qaidah New Memorization • Surah Fil, Quraish, Ma'un • Surah Kawthar • Surah Kafirun • Surah Nasr • Surah Lahab	Revision • Old students revise all surahs from Grade Qaidah to Grade 1 • New students memorize all surahs from Grade Qaidah to Grade 1 New Memorization • Surah 'Adiyat • Surah Qari'ah • Surah Takathur • Surah Asr • Surah Humazah
Kalimah and Dua Memorization	An Nasihah Surah/Du'a F1 and F2 • The first kalimah (124) * • The second kalimah (132) * • Ta'awwudh (127) * • At the time of eating, sleep (127) * • When greeting Muslim (127) * • Reply to the salam (128) * • At the time of drinking water (and reciting Quran) (128) * • Hear Messenger (s) name (133) * • When we, another sneeze (134) * • Reply sneezing person (134) • When entering washroom (135) * • When leaving washrm (135) • After eating (135) * • When forget recite at eating (136) * • When waking up (136) *	Revision • Old students revise all duas learned in Grade Qaidah • New students memorize required duas (marked *) from Grade Qaidah An Nasihah Surah and Du'a C1 • Takbir Tahrima (141) * • Dua Al-Istiftah (141) * • Tasbih of ruku (141) * • Rising from ruku (142) * • In qawmah (142) * • Tasbih of sajdah (142) * • Between two sajdah (142) • Completing the salah (143) *	Revision • Old students revise all duas learned in Grade Qaidah and Grade 1 • New students memorize required duas (marked *) from Grade Qaidah and Grade 1 An Nasihah Surah and Du'a C2 • Tashahhud (147) * • Durud Ibrahim (148) * • After Durud Ibrahim (149) * • Before wudu (150) • After wudu (150) * • Entering the masjid (151) * • Leaving the masjid (151)
Islamic Studies		New Material • Nasihah Coursebook, Workbook 1	Revision • All students revise Nasihah Coursebook 1 (except Hadith) New Material • Nasihah Coursebook, Workbook 2

	Grade 3 (Ages 8-9)	Grade 4 (Ages 9-10)	Grade 5 (Ages 10-11)
Quran Reading	Group 1 (old, studied tajwid earlier) • Quran Recitation (Juz 6-8) while asking to identify tajwid rules, 1 hour Group 2 (new, didn't study tajwid) • Join Grade 2, Group 2 for full hour *Quran Reading subject is 55-60 min. Remaining subjects are 20-30 min.*	Group 1 (old, studied tajwid earlier) • Quran Recitation (Juz 9-11) while asking to identify tajwid rules, 45 min Group 2 (new, didn't study tajwid) • Join Grade 2, Group 2 for first 45 min	Group 1 (old, studied tajwid earlier) • Quran Recitation (Juz 12-15) while asking to identify tajwid rules, 45 min Group 2 (new, didn't study tajwid) • Join Grade 2, Group 2 for first 45 min
Quran Memo-rization	<u>Revision</u> • Old students revise all surahs from Grade Qaidah to Grade 2 • New students memorize all surahs from Grade Qaidah to Grade 2 <u>New Memorization</u> • Surah Inshirah • Surah Tin • Surah Alaq • Surah Qadr • Surah Bayyinah • Surah Zilzal	<u>Revision</u> • Old students revise all surahs from Grade Qaidah to Grade 3 • New students memorize all surahs from Grade Qaidah to Grade 2 <u>New Memorization</u> • Surah Fajr • Surah Balad • Surah Shams • Surah Layl • Surah Dhuha • Ayat Al-Kursi	<u>Revision</u> • Old students revise all surahs from Grade Qaidah to Grade 4 • New students memorize all surahs from Grade Qaidah to Grade 2 <u>New Memorization</u> • Surah Yasin (first two ruku)
Kalimah and Dua Memo-rization	<u>Revision</u> • Old students revise all duas learned in Grade Qaidah, Grade 1, Grade 2 • New students memorize required duas (marked *) from Grade Qaidah, Grade 1, Grade 2 <u>An Nasihah Surah and Du'a C3</u> • Qunut (155)* • Dua to make for parent (154)* • Entering a house (154) • Leaving a house (155) • When breaking the fast (157)* • When traveling (158)* • Dua to make for host (156)	<u>Revision</u> • Old students revise all duas learned in Grade Qaidah, Grade 1, Grade 2, Grade 3 • New students memorize required duas (marked *) from Grade Qaidah, Grade 1, Grade 2, Grade 3 <u>An Nasihah Surah and Du'a C4</u> • Adhan (163)* • Extra words Fajr adhan (164)* • Reply to words of adhan (164) • After adhan (165) • Janazah dua (166)* • Janazah dua male infant (167) • Janazah dua female infant (167)	<u>Revision</u> • Old students revise all duas learned in Grade Qaidah, Grade 1, Grade 2, Grade 3, Grade 4 • New students memorize required duas (marked *) from Grade Qaidah, Grade 1, Grade 2, Grade 3, Grade 4 <u>An Nasihah Surah and Du'a C5</u> • Protection from calamities (172) • At conclusion of a gathering (173)* • When visiting the sick (174) • When in distress (175) • When feeling anger (175) • Dua at time of need (hajah) (177)* • Dua on Laylatul Qadr (172)
Islamic Studies	<u>Revision</u> • All students revise Nasihah Coursebook 1, 2 (except Hadith) <u>New Material</u> • Nasihah Coursebook, Workbook 3	<u>Revision</u> • All students revise Nasihah Coursebook 1, 2, 3 (except Hadith) <u>New Material</u> • Nasihah Coursebook, Workbook 4	<u>Revision</u> • All students revise Nasihah Coursebook 1, 2, 3, 4 (except Hadith, Akhlaq, Adab) <u>New Material</u> • Nasihah Coursebook, Workbook 5

	Grade 6 (Ages 11-12)	**Grade 7** (Ages 12-13)	**Grade 8** (Ages 13-14)
Quran Reading	• Quran recitation (assigned for individual recitation, Juz 16-20) 15 min daily	• Quran recitation (assigned for individual recitation, Juz 21-25) 15 min daily	• Quran recitation (assigned for individual recitation, 26-30) 15 min daily
Quran Memorization	Revision • Old students revise all surahs from Grade Qaidah to Grade 5 • New students memorize all surahs from Grade Qaidah to Grade 2 New Memorization • Surah Yasin (to completion)	Revision • Old students revise all surahs from Grade Qaidah to Grade 6 • New students memorize all surahs from Grade Qaidah to Grade 2	Revision • Old students revise all surahs from Grade Qaidah to Grade 6 • New students memorize all surahs from Grade Qaidah to Grade 2
Kalimah and Dua Memorization	Revision • Old students revise all duas learned in Grade Qaidah, Grade 1, Grade 2, Grade 3, Grade 4, Grade 5 • New students memorize required duas (marked *) from Grade Qaidah, Grade 1, Grade 2, Grade 3, Grade 4, Grade 5 An Nasihah Surah and Du'a C6 • Returning from journey (180) • Protection from evil eye (182)* • Sayyidul Istighfar (183)* • When in market place (184) • When having nightmare (186)*	Revision • Old students revise all duas learned in Grade Qaidah, Grade 1, Grade 2, Grade 3, Grade 4, Grade 5, Grade 6 • New students memorize required duas (marked *) from Grade Qaidah, Grade 1, Grade 2, Grade 3, Grade 4, Grade 5, Grade 6 An Nasihah Surah and Du'a C7 • Most comprehensive dua (190) • Talbiya (191) • Takbir of Tashriq (192) • When visiting graveyard (194)* • Time of burying deceased (195) • To benefit from knowledge (195) • At the time of death (196)	Revision • Old students revise all duas learned in Grade Qaidah, Grade 1, Grade 2, Grade 3, Grade 4, Grade 5, Grade 6, Grade 7 • New students memorize required duas (marked *) from Grade Qaidah, Grade 1, Grade 2, Grade 3, Grade 4, Grade 5, Grade 6, Grade 7 An Nasihah Surah and Du'a C8 • Dua for seeking guidance – Istikharah (200) • Qunut Nazilah (201) • Slaughtering an animal (203) • Asking for rain (204)
Islamic Studies	Revision • All students revise Nasihah Coursebook 4, 5 all sections (except Hadith) New Material • Nasihah Coursebook, Workbook 6	Revision • All students revise Nasihah Coursebook 5, 6 all sections (except Hadith) New Material • Nasihah Coursebook, Workbook 7	Revision • All students revise Nasihah Coursebook 7 all sections (except Hadith) New Material • Nasihah Coursebook, Workbook 8

Syllabus and Schedule: Grade Qaidah

Daily Schedule

Subject	Monday	Tuesday	Wednesday	Thursday/(Friday)
Quran Reading and Tajwid — Qaidah or Reading	50 minutes	55 minutes	55 minutes	50 minutes
Quran Memorization	10 minutes	5 minutes	5 minutes	10 minutes
Kalimah and Dua Memorization	10 minutes	10 minutes	10 minutes	10 minutes

Syllabus

Please note that for Quran Reading & Tajwid, the textbook used is **Safar Complete Qa'idah**. Levels referred to reference levels, or chapters, of the Safar Qaidah. For Dua Memorization, the kalimahs and duas referenced are in the **An-Nasihah Islamic Curriculum Surah and Du'a** book. Note that one class in Grade Qaidah can have two groups (at different levels of the qaidah) in Quran Reading & Tajwid. Completion status for each of these two groups can be tracked separately.

Trim-Week	Start Date	Quran Reading & Tajwid	Quran Memorization	Dua Memorization
1-1 (1)		• Complete Student Introductions, Fill Out Necessary Information in Class Register (Student Full Name, Parent Name, Phone Number, Medical Info) • Conduct Motivational Sessions and Train Students in Class Rules and Etiquette. Review the Student Code of Conduct. • Administer Placement Exam to All Students and Place Students in Coordination with Other Teachers		
1-2 (2)		• Level 1: Letter recognition first 11 letters with attention to correct letter makharij • Documentation: Quran Reading Rubric (makharij) Weeks 1-6, Comprehensive Assess. Group 1 Complete☐ Group 2 Complete☐	• Memorization: Surah Fatihah • Documentation: Comprehensive Assessment Complete☐	• Memorization: First Kalimah with meaning • Documentation: Comprehensive Assessment Complete☐
1-3 (3)		Level 1: Letter recognition first 11 letters with attention to correct letter makharij Group 1 Complete☐ Group 2 Complete☐	Memorization: Surah Fatihah	Memorization: First Kalimah with meaning
1-4 (4)		Level 1: Letter recognition all 23 letters with attention to correct letter makharij Group 1 Complete☐ Group 2 Complete☐	Memorization: Surah Fatihah	Memorization: First Kalimah with meaning
1-5 (5)		Level 2: Letter recognition all 29 letters with attention to correct letter makharij Group 1 Complete☐ Group 2 Complete☐	Memorization: Surah Fatihah	Memorization: Second kalimah with meaning
1-6 (6)		• Level 2: Mixed Alphabet with attention to correct letter makharij • Documentation: Quran Reading Rubric (makharij) Weeks 1-6	Memorization: Surah Fatihah	Memorization: Second kalimah with meaning

#			
1-7 (7)	Level 2: Assorted letters with attention to correct letter makharij Documentation: Quran Reading Rubric (makharij) Weeks 7-12, Comprehensive Assess Group 1 Complete☐ Group 2 Complete☐	Group 1 Complete☐ Group 2 Complete☐	• Memorization: Second Kalimah with meaning • Documentation: Comprehensive Assessment Complete☐
1-8 (8)	Level 2: Assorted letters with attention to correct letter makharij Group 1 Complete☐ Group 2 Complete☐	Memorization: Surah Fatihah Complete☐	• Memorization: Dua before eating, Taawudh and Tasmiyah • Revision: Previously memorized kalimahs, duas Complete☐
1-9 (9)	Level 2: Assorted Joined letters with attention to correct letter makharij Group 1 Complete☐ Group 2 Complete☐	Memorization: Surah Fatihah Complete☐	• Memorization: Dua before eating, Taawudh and Tasmiyah • Revision: Previously memorized kalimahs, duas Complete☐
1-10 (10)	Level 2: First words, letter recognition with attention to correct letter makharij Group 1 Complete☐ Group 2 Complete☐	• Memorization: Surah Ikhlas • Revision: Surah Fatihah Complete☐	• Memorization: Dua before eating, Taawudh and Tasmiyah • Revision: Previously memorized kalimahs, duas Complete☐
1-11 (11)	Level 2: Letter recognition Group 1 Complete☐ Group 2 Complete☐	• Memorization: Surah Ikhlas • Revision: Surah Fatihah Complete☐	• Memorization: Dua if you forgot to recite before eating • Revision: Previously memorized kalimahs, duas Complete☐
1-12 (12)	• Level 2: Letter recognition • Documentation: Quran Reading Rubric (makharij) Weeks 7-12, Comprehensive Assessment, Report Card Group 1 Complete☐ Group 2 Complete☐	• Memorization: Surah Ikhlas • Revision: Surah Fatihah • Documentation: Comprehensive Assessment, Report Card Complete☐	• Memorization: Dua if you forgot to recite before eating • Documentation: Comprehensive Assessment, Report Card Complete☐
2-1 (13)	• Level 3: Fluency in spelling whole word • Documentation: Quran Reading Rubric (makharij) Weeks 1-6 Group 1 Complete☐ Group 2 Complete☐	• Memorization: Surah Ikhlas • Revision: Surah Fatihah Complete☐	• Memorization: Dua after eating • Revision: Previously memorized kalimahs, duas Complete☐
2-2 (14)	Level 3: Fluency in spelling whole word Group 1 Complete☐ Group 2 Complete☐	• Memorization: Surah Ikhlas • Revision: Surah Fatihah Complete☐	• Memorization: Dua after eating • Revision: Previously memorized kalimahs, duas Complete☐
2-3 (15)	Level: 4 Advanced letter recognition Group 1 Complete☐ Group 2 Complete☐	• Memorization: Surah Ikhlas • Revision: Surah Fatihah Complete☐	• Memorization: Dua after eating • Revision: Previously memorized kalimahs, duas Complete☐
2-4 (16)	Level: 4 Advanced Letter recognition Group 1 Complete☐ Group 2 Complete☐	• Memorization: Surah Ikhlas • Revision: Surah Fatihah Complete☐	• Memorization: Dua befor entering the washroom, leaving the washroom • Revision: Previously memorized kalimahs, duas Complete☐

#	Column 2	Column 3	Column 4
2-5 (17)	Level: 5a Harakahs Fathah, Kasrah Group 1 Complete☐ Group 2 Complete☐	• Memorization: Surah Nas • Revision: Previously memorized surahs Complete☐	• Memorization: Dua before entering the washroom, leaving the washroom • Revision: Previously memorized kalimahs, duas Complete☐
2-6 (18)	• Level:5a Dammah, Advanced pronunciation practice • Documentation: Quran Reading Rubric (makharij) Weeks 1-6 Group 1 Complete☐ Group 2 Complete☐	• Memorization: Surah Nas • Revision: Previously memorized surahs Complete☐	• Memorization: Dua before entering the washroom, leaving the washroom • Revision: Previously memorized kalimahs, duas Complete☐
2-7 (19)	• Level:5a Dammah, Advanced pronunciation practice • Documentation: Quran Reading Rubric (makharij) Weeks 7-12, Comprehensive Assess Group 1 Complete☐ Group 2 Complete☐	• Memorization: Surah Nas • Revision: Previously memorized surahs • Documentation: Comprehensive Assessment Complete☐	• Memorization: Dua of sleeping • Revision: Previously memorized kalimahs, duas • Documentation: Comprehensive Assessment Complete☐
2-8 (20)	Level 5b: Tanwin Group 1 Complete☐ Group 2 Complete☐	• Memorization: Surah Nas • Revision: Previously memorized surahs Complete☐	• Memorization: Dua of sleeping • Revision: Previously memorized kalimahs, duas Complete☐
2-9 (21)	Level 5b: Tanwin Group 1 Complete☐ Group 2 Complete☐	• Memorization: Surah Nas • Revision: Previously memorized surahs Complete☐	• Memorization: Dua of sleeping • Revision: Previously memorized kalimahs, duas Complete☐
2-10 (22)	Level 6a: Stretched Harakahs Group 1 Complete☐ Group 2 Complete☐	• Memorization: Surah Nas • Revision: Previously memorized surahs Complete☐	• Memorization: Dua of waking up • Revision: Previously memorized kalimahs, duas Complete☐
2-11 (23)	Level 6b: Long Harakah Group 1 Complete☐ Group 2 Complete☐	• Memorization: Surah Nas • Revision: Previously memorized surahs Complete☐	• Memorization: Dua of waking up • Revision: Previously memorized kalimahs, duas Complete☐
2-12 (24)	• Level 6c: Lin (Fathah followed by joining Ya) • Documentation: Quran Reading Rubric (makharij) Weeks 7-12, Comprehensive Assessment, Report Card Group 1 Complete☐ Group 2 Complete☐	• Revision: Surahs Fatihah, Ikhlas, Nas • Documentation: Comprehensive Assessment, Report Card Complete☐	• Memorization: Dua of waking up • Revision: Previously memorized kalimahs, duas • Documentation: Comprehensive Assessment, Report Card Complete☐
3-1 (25)	• Level 7: Joining Letters with sukun • Documentation: Quran Reading Rubric (makharij) Weeks 1-6 Group 1 Complete☐ Group 2 Complete☐	• Memorization: Surah Falaq • Revision: Previously memorized surahs Complete☐	• Memorization: Dua at the time of drinking water and reciting Quran • Revision: Previously memorized kalimahs, duas Complete☐
3-2 (26)	Level 7: Joining Letters with Shaddah Group 1 Complete☐ Group 2 Complete☐	• Memorization: Surah Falaq • Revision: Previously memorized surahs Complete☐	• Memorization: Dua at the time of drinking water and reciting Quran • Revision: Previously memorized kalimahs, duas Complete☐

#	Level / Topic	Memorization / Revision
3-3 (27)	Level 8: Madd Group 1 Complete☐ Group 2 Complete☐	• Memorization: Surah Falaq • Revision: Previously memorized surahs Complete☐	• Memorization: Dua at the time of drinking water and reciting Quran • Revision: Previously memorized kalimahs, duas Complete☐
3-4 (28)	Level 9: Special Cases Group 1 Complete☐ Group 2 Complete☐	• Memorization: Surah Falaq • Revision: Previously memorized surahs Complete☐	• Memorization: Dua when we sneeze, when another person sneezes, reply sneezing person • Revision: Previously memorized kalimahs, duas Complete☐
3-5 (29)	Level 10: Fluency in three words Group 1 Complete☐ Group 2 Complete☐	• Memorization: Surah Falaq • Revision: Previously memorized surahs Complete☐	• Memorization: Dua when we sneeze, when another person sneezes, reply sneezing person • Revision: Previously memorized kalimahs, duas Complete☐
3-6 (30)	• Level 10: Fluency in three words • Documentation: Quran Reading Rubric (makharij) Weeks 1-6 Group 1 Complete☐ Group 2 Complete☐	• Memorization: Surah Falaq • Revision: Previously memorized surahs Complete☐	• Memorization: Dua when we sneeze, when another person sneezes, reply sneezing person • Revision: Previously memorized kalimahs, duas Complete☐
3-7 (31)	• Level 11: Stopping • Documentation: Quran Reading Rubric (makharij) Weeks 7-12, Comprehensive Assess Group 1 Complete☐ Group 2 Complete☐	• Memorization: Surah Falaq • Revision: Previously memorized surahs • Documentation: Comprehensive Assessment Complete☐	• Memorization: Dua when greeting Muslim, reply to salaam, when hear messenger's name • Revision: Previously memorized kalimahs, duas • Documentation: Comprehensive Assessment Complete☐
3-8 (32)	Level 11: Stopping, Rules on stopping fathatayn, round Ta, Ha, all other stops Group 1 Complete☐ Group 2 Complete☐	Revision: Surahs Fatihah, Ikhlas, Falaq, Nas Complete☐	• Memorization: Dua when greeting Muslim, reply to salaam, when hear messenger's name • Revision: Previously memorized kalimahs, duas Complete☐
3-9 (33)	Level 12: Stopping Symbols Group 1 Complete☐ Group 2 Complete☐	Revision: Surahs Fatihah, Ikhlas, Falaq, Nas Complete☐	• Memorization: Dua when greeting Muslim, reply to salaam, when hear messenger's name • Revision: Previously memorized kalimahs, duas Complete☐
3-10 (34)	Level 13: Fluency in one line or verse Group 1 Complete☐ Group 2 Complete☐	Revision: Surahs Fatihah, Ikhlas, Falaq, Nas Complete☐	Revision: Previously memorized kalimahs, duas Complete☐
3-11 (35)	Overview of Qaidah using supplementary exercises Group 1 Complete☐ Group 2 Complete☐	Revision: Surahs Fatihah, Ikhlas, Falaq, Nas Complete☐	Revision: Previously memorized kalimahs, duas Complete☐
3-12 (36)	• Overview of Qaidah using supplementary exercises • Documentation: Quran Reading Rubric (makharij) Weeks 7-12, Comprehensive Assess, Report Card Group 1 Complete☐ Group 2 Complete☐	• Revision: Surahs Fatihah, Ikhlas, Falaq, Nas • Documentation: Comprehensive Assessment, Report Card Complete☐	• Revision: previously memorized kalimahs, duas • Documentation: Comprehensive Assessment, Report Card Complete☐

Syllabus and Schedule: Grade 1

Daily Schedule

This schedule assumes 7-10 students in a class. If there are less, increase the number of lines recited daily for Quran Reading and Tajwid within the same 30 minutes allocated to Reading. If there are more students, class time must be increased beyond the suggested 70 minutes total, or the class may be split into two classes.

Subject	Monday	Tuesday	Wednesday	Thursday/(Friday)
Quran Reading and Tajwid				
Qaidah or Reading	30 minutes	30 minutes	30 minutes	30 minutes
Tajwid	20 minutes	10 minutes	10 minutes	10 minutes
Quran Memorization	10 minutes	10 minutes	15 minutes	
Kalimah and Dua Memorization		15 minutes		15 minutes
Islamic Studies	10 minutes	15 minutes	15 minutes	15 minutes

Syllabus

In Quran Reading & Tajwid, the tajwid rules referenced are from the book **Safar Rules of Tajwid**. In Dua Memorization, the duas listed are from the book **An Nasihah Islamic Curriculum Surah & Du'a**. In Islamic Studies, lessons listed are from the book **An Nasihah Islamic Curriculum Grade 1 Coursebook**. Students should also purchase the associated Workbook along with the coursebook.

Trim-Week	Start Date	Quran Reading & Tajwid	Quran Memorization	Dua Memorization	Islamic Studies
1-1 (1)		• Complete Student Introductions and Fill Out Necessary Information in Class Register (Student Full Name, Parent Name, Phone Number, Medical Info) • Conduct Motivational Sessions and Train Students in Class Rules and Etiquette. Revision: the Student Code of Conduct. • Administer Placement Exam to All Students • Start Completing Comprehensive Assessments for All Students.			
1-2 (2)		• Recitation: Juz 1 (3+ lines daily) • Safar Complete Qaidah (Levels 1-5) Review: Pronunciation, Letter Recognition, Harakah • Practice Makharij (ح، ث) • Documentation: Quran Reading Rubric, Comprehensive Assessment Complete☐	• Recitation: Surah Fatihah • Documentation: Comprehensive Assessment Complete☐	• Revision: First kalimah with translation • Documentation: Comprehensive Assessment Complete☐	• Aqaid: Articles of Faith • Aqaid: Allah is Razzaq • Documentation: Comprehensive Assessment Complete☐
1-3 (3)		• Recitation: Juz 1 (3+ lines daily) • Safar Complete Qaidah (Levels 6-8) Review Stretched Harakahs, Joining Letters, Madd • Practice Makharij (ذ، ث) Complete☐	Revision: Surah Fatihah Complete☐	Revision: Second kalimah with translation Complete☐	Aqaid: Allah is Rehman Complete☐

1-4 (4)	• Recitation: Juz 1 (3+ lines daily) • Safar Complete Qaidah (Levels 9-13) Review: Special Case, Stopping • Practice Makharij (ص ض) Complete ☐	Revision: Surah Ikhlas Complete ☐	• Revision: Dua for when reciting Quran • Revision: Ta'awwudh Complete ☐	Review and Test: Aqaid Chapter Complete ☐
1-5 (5)	• Recitation: Juz 1 (3+ lines daily) • Practice Makharij (ط ظ) • Level 14 (Safar Rules of Tajwid): Ta'awwudh and Basmalah Complete ☐	Revision: Surah Ikhlas Complete ☐	• Memorization: Takbir Tahrima • Memorization: Dua al-Istiftah Complete ☐	Fiqh: 5 Pillars of Islam, Shahadah Complete ☐
1-6 (6)	• Recitation: Juz 1 (3+ lines daily) • Practice Makharij (خ غ) • Level 15: Mim Mushaddadah and Nun Mushaddadah Complete ☐	Revision: Surah Falaq Complete ☐	Memorization: Tasbih of ruku Complete ☐	Fiqh: 5 Pillars of Islam, Salah Complete ☐
1-7 (7)	• Recitation: Juz 1 (4+ lines daily) • Level 16: Qalqalah Complete ☐	Revision: Surah Falaq Complete ☐	• Memorization: Dua when rising from ruku • Memorization: Dua Qawmah Complete ☐	Fiqh: Taharah Complete ☐
1-8 (8)	• Recitation: Juz 1 (4+ lines daily) • Level L17a: Tafkhim: Lam of Allah Complete ☐	Revision: Surah Nas Complete ☐	Memorization: Tasbih of Sajdah Complete ☐	Fiqh: Wudu Complete ☐
1-9 (9)	• Recitation: Juz 1 (4+ lines daily) • Level 17b: Tafkhim: Ra Mutaharrikah Complete ☐	Revision: Surah Nas Complete ☐	Memorization: Tasbih read between two sajdah Complete ☐	Fiqh: 5 Pillars of Islam, Zakah Complete ☐
1-10 (10)	• Recitation: Juz 1 (4+ lines daily) • Level 17c: Tafkhim: Ra Sakinah Complete ☐	Memorization: Surah Nasr Complete ☐	Memorization: Dua for completing salah Complete ☐	Fiqh: 5 Pillars of Islam, Sawm Complete ☐
1-11 (11)	• Recitation: Juz 1 (4+ lines daily) • Review: Levels 14-17c Complete ☐	Memorization: Surah Nasr Complete ☐	• Memorization: Dua for completing salah • Revision: All Previous Duas Complete ☐	Fiqh: 5 Pillars of Islam, Hajj Complete ☐
1-12 (12)	• Recitation: Juz 1 (5+ lines daily) • Level 17d: Tafkhim: Full mouth letters • Documentation: Quran Reading Rubric, Comprehensive Assessment Complete ☐	• Revision: All Previous Surahs • Documentation: Comprehensive Assessment Complete ☐	• Revision: All Previous Duas • Documentation: Comprehensive Assessment Complete ☐	• Review and Test: Fiqh Chapter • Documentation: Comprehensive Assessment Complete ☐
2-1 (13)	• Recitation: Juz 1 (5+ lines daily) • Level 17e: Tafkhim: Alif Complete ☐	Memorization: Surah Kawthar Complete ☐	Revision: All Previous Duas Complete ☐	Ahadith: Truth Complete ☐

2-2 (14)	• Recitation: Juz 1 (5+ lines daily) • Level 18a: Mim Sakinah: Ikhfa Shafawi Complete ☐	Memorization: Surah Kawthar Complete ☐	Revision: Dua for when greeting Muslim Complete ☐	Ahadith: Feeding the hungry Complete ☐
2-3 (15)	• Recitation: Juz 1 (5+ lines daily) • Level 18b: Mim Sakinah: Idgham Shafawi Complete ☐	Memorization: Surah Lahab Complete ☐	Revision: The reply to salam Complete ☐	Ahadith: Helping others Complete ☐
2-4 (16)	• Recitation: Juz 1 (5+ lines daily) • Level 18c: Mim Sakinah: Izhar Shafawi Complete ☐	Memorization: Surah Lahab Complete ☐	• Revision: Dua for when we or another sneeze • Revision: Dua for replying to a sneezing person Complete ☐	Ahadith: Doing things slowly Complete ☐
2-5 (17)	• Recitation: Juz 1 (6+ lines daily) • Review: Levels 14 - 18 Complete ☐	Memorization: Surah Lahab Complete ☐	Revision: Dua at time of eating Complete ☐	Ahadith: Cleanliness Complete ☐
2-6 (18)	• Recitation: Juz 1 (6+ lines daily) • Level 19a: Nun Sakinah and Tanwin: Qalb Complete ☐	Revision: All Previous Surahs Complete ☐	Revision: Dua when you forget to recite at time of eating Complete ☐	Review and Test: Ahadith Chapter Complete ☐
2-7 (19)	• Recitation: Juz 1 (6+ lines daily) • Level 19b: Nun Sakinah and Tanwin: Idgham without ghunnah Complete ☐	Memorization: Surah Kafirun Complete ☐	Revision: All Previous Duas Complete ☐	Akhlaq: Cleanliness Complete ☐
2-8 (20)	• Recitation: Juz 1 (6+ lines daily) • Level 19c: Nun Sakinah and Tanwin: Idgham with ghunnah Complete ☐	Memorization: Surah Kafirun Complete ☐	Revision: All Previous Duas Complete ☐	Akhlaq: Respect Complete ☐
2-9 (21)	• Recitation: Juz 1 (6+ lines daily) • Level 19d: Nun Sakinah and Tanwin: Izhar Complete ☐	Memorization: Surah Kafirun Complete ☐	Revision: All Previous Duas Complete ☐	Akhlaq: Smiling Complete ☐
2-10 (22)	• Recitation: Juz 1 (7+ lines daily) • Level 19e: Nun Sakinah and Tanwin: Ikhfa Complete ☐	Memorization: Surah Ma'un Complete ☐	Revision: All Previous Duas Complete ☐	Akhlaq: Gentleness in Speech Complete ☐
2-11 (23)	• Recitation: Juz 1 (7+ lines daily) • Review: Levels 14 - 19 Complete ☐	Memorization: Surah Ma'un Complete ☐	Revision: All Previous Duas Complete ☐	Akhlaq: Beginning from right side Complete ☐
2-12 (24)	• Recitation: Juz 1 (7+ lines daily) • Level 20a: Madd: Madd Muttasil • Documentation: Quran Reading Rubric, Comprehensive Assessment Complete ☐	• Memorization: Surah Ma'un • Documentation: Comprehensive Assessment Complete ☐	• Revision: All Previous Duas • Documentation: Comprehensive Assessment Complete ☐	• Review and Test: Akhlaq chapter • Documentation: Comprehensive Assessment Complete ☐

#	Recitation/Tajweed	Memorization/Surahs	Duas	Islamic Studies
3-1	• Recitation: Juz 1 (7+ lines daily) • Level 20b: Madd: Madd Munfasil Complete ☐	Revision: All Previous Surahs Complete ☐	• Revision: Dua for after eating • Revision: Dua drinking water Complete ☐	Adab: Eating Adab: Drinking Complete ☐
3-2	• Recitation: Juz 1 (7+ lines daily) • L20c: Madd: Madd Arid Complete ☐	Memorization: Surah Quraish Complete ☐	• Revision: Dua when sleeping • Revision: Dua when waking up Complete ☐	Adab: Sleeping Adab: Waking up Complete ☐
3-3	• Recitation: Juz 1 (8+ lines daily) • Level 20d: Madd: Madd Lazim Complete ☐	Memorization: Surah Quraish Complete ☐	• Revision: Dua entering washroom • Revision: Dua leaving washroom Complete ☐	Adab: Using the washroom Complete ☐
3-4	• Recitation: Juz 1 (8+ lines daily) • Level 20e: Madd: Madd Asli Complete ☐	Memorization: Surah Quraish Complete ☐	Revision: All Previous Duas Complete ☐	Review and Test: Adab Chapter Complete ☐
3-5	• Recitation: Juz 1 (8+ lines daily) • Review Levels 14 - 20 Complete ☐	Memorization: Surah Fil Complete ☐	Revision: All Previous Duas Complete ☐	Sirah Complete ☐
3-6	• Recitation: Juz 1 (8+ lines daily) • Review Levels 14 - 20 Complete ☐	Memorization: Surah Fil Complete ☐	Revision: Durood for when you hear Messenger (S) name Complete ☐	Sirah Complete ☐
3-7	• Recitation: Juz 1 (8+ lines daily) • Review Levels 14 - 20 Complete ☐	Memorization: Surah Fil Complete ☐	Revision: All Previous Duas Complete ☐	Review and Test: Sirah chapter Complete ☐
3-8	• Recitation: Juz 1 (9+ lines daily) • Review Levels 14 - 20 Complete ☐	Revision: All Previous Surahs Complete ☐	Revision: All Previous Duas Complete ☐	Tarikh: Adam (a) Complete ☐
3-9	• Recitation: Juz 1 (9+ lines daily) • Review Levels 14 - 20 Complete ☐	Revision: All Previous Surahs Complete ☐	Revision: All Previous Duas Complete ☐	Tarikh: Nuh (a) Complete ☐
3-10	• Recitation: Juz 1 (10+ lines daily) Complete ☐	Revision: All Previous Surahs Complete ☐	Revision: All Previous Duas Complete ☐	Tarikh: Nuh (a) Complete ☐
3-11	• Recitation: Juz 1 (11+ lines daily) Complete ☐	Revision: All Previous Surahs Complete ☐	Revision: All Previous Duas Complete ☐	Review and Test: Tarikh chapter Complete ☐
3-12	• Recitation: Juz 1 (11+ lines daily) • Documentation: Quran Reading Rubric, Comprehensive Assessment Complete ☐	• Revision: All Previous Surahs • Documentation: Comprehensive Assessment Complete ☐	• Revision: All Previous Duas • Documentation: Comprehensive Assessment Complete ☐	• Review: All Islamic Studies • Documentation: Comprehensive Assessment Complete ☐

Syllabus and Schedule: Grade 2

Daily Schedule

This schedule assumes 7-10 students in a class. If there are less, increase the number of lines recited daily for Quran Reading and Tajwid within the same 30 minutes allocated to Reading. If there are more students, class time must be increased beyond the suggested 70 minutes total, or the class may be split into two classes.

Subject	Monday	Tuesday	Wednesday	Thursday/(Friday)
Quran Reading and Tajwid				
Qaidah or Reading	30 minutes	30 minutes	30 minutes	30 minutes
Tajwid	20 minutes	10 minutes	10 minutes	10 minutes
Quran Memorization	10 minutes	15 minutes	15 minutes	
Kalimah and Dua Memorization		15 minutes		15 minutes
Islamic Studies	10 minutes	15 minutes	15 minutes	15 minutes

Syllabus

In Quran Reading & Tajwid, the tajwid rules referenced are from the book **Safar Rules of Tajwid**. In Dua Memorization, the duas listed are from the book **An Nasihah Islamic Curriculum Surah & Du'a**. In Islamic Studies, lessons listed are from the book **An Nasihah Islamic Curriculum Grade 2 Coursebook**. Students should also purchase the associated Workbook along with the coursebook.

Trim-Week	Start Date	Quran Reading & Tajwid	Quran Memorization	Dua Memorization	Islamic Studies
1-1 (1)		• Complete Student Introductions and Fill Out Necessary Information in Class Register (Student Full Name, Parent Name, Phone Number, Medical Info) • Conduct Motivational Sessions and Train Students in Class Rules and Etiquette. Revision: the Student Code of Conduct. • Administer Placement Exam to All Students • Start Completing Comprehensive Assessments for All Students.			
1-2 (2)		• Recitation Juz 3-6 (6+ lines daily) • Practice Makharij (ت، ث) • Documentation: Quran Reading Rubric, Comprehensive Assessment Complete ☐	• Revision: Surah Fatihah • Documentation: Comprehensive Assessment Complete ☐	• Revision: First and Second Kalimah with translation • Documentation: Comprehensive Assessment Complete ☐	• Revision: An Nasihah Islamic Curriculum Grade 1: Aqaid • Documentation: Comprehensive Assessment Complete ☐
1-3 (3)		• Recitation Juz 3-6 (6+ lines daily) • Practice Makharij (ق، ذ) Complete ☐	• Revision: Surahs Ikhlas, Falaq	• Revision: Dua for when reciting Quran • Revision: Ta'awwudh Complete ☐	• Revision: An Nasihah Islamic Curriculum Grade 1: Fiqh Complete ☐
1-4 (4)		• Recitation Juz 3-6 (7+ lines daily) • Practice Makharij (خ، ح)	• Revision: Surahs Falaq, Nas	• Revision: Takbir Tahrima • Revision: Dua al-Istiftah	• Revision: An Nasihah Islamic Curriculum Grade 1: Fiqh

	• Level 14 (Safar Rules of Tajweed): Ta'awwudh and Basmalah Complete ☐			
1-5 (5)	• Recitation Juz 3-6 (7+ lines daily) • Practice Makharij (ط، ظ) • Level 15: Mim Mushaddadah and Nun Mushaddadah Complete ☐	• Revision: Surah Fil, Quraish Complete ☐	• Revision: Tasbih of ruku • Memorization: Tashahhud Complete ☐	• Revision: An Nasihah Islamic Curriculum Grade 1: Sirah • Revision: An Nasihah Islamic Curriculum Grade 1: Tarikh Complete ☐
1-6 (6)	• Recitation Juz 3-6 (7+ lines daily) • Practice Makharij (ج، ح) • Level 16: Qalqalah Complete ☐	• Revision: Surah Ma'un Complete ☐	• Revision: Dua when rising from Ruku • Revision: Dua in Qawmah • Memorization: Tashahhud Complete ☐	• Revision: An Nasihah Islamic Curriculum Grade 1: Akhlaq • Revision: An Nasihah Islamic Curriculum Grade 1: Adab Complete ☐
1-7 (7)	• Recitation Juz 3-6 (7+ lines daily) • Level 17a: Tafkhim: Lam of Allah Complete ☐	• Revision: Surah Kawthar Complete ☐	• Revision: Tasbih of Sajdah • Memorization: Tashahhud Complete ☐	• Aqaid (An Nasihah Islamic Curriculum Grade 2): Allah is Al-Hafiz Complete ☐
1-8 (8)	• Recitation Juz 3-6 (8+ lines daily) • Level 17b: Tafkhim: Ra Mutaharrik Complete ☐	• Revision: Surah Kafirun Complete ☐	• Revision: Tasbih read between two sajdah (not new students) • Memorization: Tashahhud Complete ☐	• Aqaid: Allah is As-Sami' • Aqaid: Allah is Al-Basir Complete ☐
1-9 (9)	• Recitation Juz 3-6 (8+ lines daily) • Level 17c: Tafkhim: Ra Sakina Complete ☐	• Revision: Surah Nasr Complete ☐	• Revision: Dua for completing salah • Memorization: Durud Ibrahim Complete ☐	• Aqaid: Angels Complete ☐
1-10 (10)	• Recitation Juz 3-6 (8+ lines daily) • Review: Levels 14-17c Complete ☐	• Revision: Surah Lahab Complete ☐	• Revision: Dua for Completing Salah • Memorization: Durud Ibrahim • Revision: All Previous Duas Complete ☐	• Aqaid: Revealed Books • Aqaid: The Quran Complete ☐
1-11 (11)	• Recitation Juz 3-6 (8+ lines daily) • Level 17d: Tafkhim: Full mouth letters Complete ☐	• Revision: All Previous Surahs Complete ☐	• Memorization: Durud Ibrahim • Revision: All Previous Duas Complete ☐	• Review and Test: Aqaid Chapter Complete ☐
1-12 (12)	• Recitation Juz 3-6 (9+ lines daily) • Level 17e: Tafkhim: Alif • Documentation: Quran Reading Rubric, Comprehensive Assessment Complete ☐	• Revision: All Previous Surahs • Documentation: Comprehensive Assessment Complete ☐	• Memorization: Durud Ibrahim • Revision: All Previous Duas • Documentation: Comprehensive Assessment Complete ☐	• Tarikh: Story of Hud (a) • Documentation: Comprehensive Assessment Complete ☐
2-1 (13)	• Recitation Juz 3-6 (9+ lines daily) • Level 18a: Mim Sakinah: Ikhfa Shafawi Complete ☐	• Memorization: Surah 'Adiyat Complete ☐	• Revision: Dua greeting Muslim • Memorization: After Durud Complete ☐	• Tarikh: Story of Salih (a) Complete ☐

#	Recitation / Tajweed	Memorization / Duas	Topics
2-2 (14)	• Recitation Juz 3-6 (9+ lines daily) • Level 18b: Mim Sakinah: Idghaam Shafawi Complete ☐	• Memorization: Surah 'Adiyat Complete ☐	• Revision: The reply to salam • Memorization: After Durud Complete ☐	• Review and Test: Tarikh Chapter Complete ☐
2-3 (15)	• Recitation Juz 3-6 (10+ lines daily) • Level 18c: Mim Sakinah: Izhar Shafawi Complete ☐	• Memorization: Surah 'Adiyat Complete ☐	• Revision: Dua for when sneeze • Revision: Dua another sneezes • Memorization: After Durud Complete ☐	• Sirah: In the Cave of Hira' • Sirah: The First Revelation • Sirah: Open Call to Islam Complete ☐
2-4 (16)	• Recitation Juz 3-6 (10+ lines daily) • Review: Levels 14-18 Complete ☐	• Memorization: Surah 'Adiyat Complete ☐	• Revision: Dua at time of eating • Memorization: After Durud Complete ☐	• Sirah: Persecutions Faced by Muslims • Review & Test: Sirah Chapter Complete ☐
2-5 (17)	• Recitation Juz 3-6 (10+ lines daily) • Level 19a: Nun Sakinah and Tanwin: Qalb Complete ☐	• Memorization: Surah Qari'ah Complete ☐	• Revision: Dua when you forget to recite at time of eating • Memorization: Before Wudu Complete ☐	• Fiqh: Istinja • Fiqh: Wudhu • Fiqh: Ghusl Complete ☐
2-6 (18)	• Recitation Juz 3-6 (10+ lines daily) • Level 19b: Nun Sakinah and Tanwin: Idgham without ghunnah Complete ☐	• Memorization: Surah Qari'ah Complete ☐	• Revision: All Previous Duas • Memorization: After Wudu Complete ☐	• Fiqh: Wudhu in Detail Complete ☐
2-7 (19)	• Recitation Juz 3-6 (11+ lines daily) • Level 19c: Nun Sakinah and Tanwin: Idgham with ghunnah Complete ☐	• Memorization: Surah Qari'ah Complete ☐	• Revision: All Previous Duas • Memorization: Entering the Masjid Complete ☐	• Fiqh: Tayammum Complete ☐
2-8 (20)	• Recitation Juz 3-6 (11+ lines daily) • Level 19d: Nun Sakinah and Tanwin: Izhar Complete ☐	• Memorization: Surah Qari'ah Complete ☐	• Revision: All Previous Duas • Memorization: Entering Masjid Complete ☐	• Fiqh: Method of Salah Complete ☐
2-9 (21)	• Recitation Juz 3-6 (11+ lines daily) • Level 19e: Nun Sakinah and Tanwin: Ikhfa Complete ☐	• Memorization: Surah Asr Complete ☐	• Revision: All Previous Duas • Memorization: Leaving Masjid Complete ☐	• Review and Test: Fiqh Chapter Complete ☐
2-10 (22)	• Recitation Juz 3-6 (11+ lines daily) • Review: Levels 14-19 Complete ☐	• Memorization: Surah Asr Complete ☐	• Revision: All Previous Duas • Memorization: Leaving Masjid Complete ☐	• Ahadith: Truth Complete ☐
2-11 (23)	• Recitation Juz 3-6 (12+ lines daily) • Level 20a: Madd: Madd Mutassil Complete ☐	• Revision: All Previous Surahs Complete ☐	• Revision: All Previous Duas Complete ☐	• Ahadith: Salam Complete ☐
2-12 (24)	• Recitation Juz 3-6 (12+ lines daily) • Level 20b: Madd: Madd Munfasil • Documentation: Quran Reading Rubric, Comprehensive Assessment Complete ☐	• Revision: All Previous Surahs • Documentation: Comprehensive Assessment Complete ☐	• Revision: All Previous Duas • Documentation: Comprehensive Assessment Complete ☐	• Ahadith: Using the Right Hand • Ahadith: Drinking While Sitting Complete ☐

#	Recitation	Memorization	Revision (Dua)	Topic
3-1 (25)	• Recitation Juz 3-6 (12+ lines daily) • Level 20c: Madd: Madd Arid Complete ☐	• Memorization: Surah Takathur Complete ☐	• Revision: Dua for after eating • Revision: Dua drinking water Complete ☐	• Ahadith: Kindness to Neighbors Complete ☐
3-2 (26)	• Recitation Juz 3-6 (12+ lines daily) • Level 20d: Madd: Madd Lazim Complete ☐	• Memorization: Surah Takathur Complete ☐	• Revision: Dua when sleeping • Revision: Dua when waking up Complete ☐	• Review and Test: Ahadith Chapter Complete ☐
3-3 (27)	• Recitation Juz 3-6 (13+ lines daily) • Level 20e: Madd: Madd Asli Complete ☐	• Memorization: Surah Takathur Complete ☐	• Revision: Dua enter washroom • Revision: Dua leave washroom Complete ☐	• Akhlaq: Keeping Promises • Akhlaq: Being Thankful Complete ☐
3-4 (28)	• Recitation Juz 3-6 (13+ lines daily) • Review Levels: 14-20 Complete ☐	• Memorization: Surah Takathur Complete ☐	• Revision: All Previous Duas Complete ☐	• Akhlaq: Spreading Salam • Akhlaq: Helping in Good Things Complete ☐
3-5 (29)	• Recitation Juz 3-6 (13+ lines daily) • Review Levels: 14-20 Complete ☐	• Memorization: Surah Humazah Complete ☐	• Revision: All Previous Duas Complete ☐	• Akhlaq: Kindness to Animals • Review and Test: Akhlaq Chapter Complete ☐
3-6 (30)	• Recitation Juz 3-6 (13+ lines daily) • Review Levels: 14-20 Complete ☐	• Memorization: Surah Humazah Complete ☐	• Revision: Durood when you hear Messenger (s) name Complete ☐	• Adab: Greeting • Adab: Entering a House Complete ☐
3-7 (31)	• Recitation Juz 3-6 (14+ lines daily) • Review Levels: 14-20 Complete ☐	• Memorization: Surah Humazah Complete ☐	• Revision: All Previous Duas Complete ☐	• Adab: Speaking Complete ☐
3-8 (32)	• Recitation Juz 3-6 (14+ lines daily) • Review Levels: 14-20 Complete ☐	• Memorization: Surah Humazah Complete ☐	• Revision: All Previous Duas Complete ☐	• Adab: Sneezing Complete ☐
3-9 (33)	• Recitation Juz 3-6 (15+ lines daily) Complete ☐	• Revision: All Previous Surahs Complete ☐	• Revision: All Previous Duas Complete ☐	• Adab: Yawning Complete ☐
3-10 (34)	• Recitation Juz 3-6 (15+ lines daily) Complete ☐	• Revision: All Previous Surahs Complete ☐	• Revision: All Previous Dua Complete ☐	• Review and Test: Adab Chapter Complete ☐
3-11 (35)	• Recitation Juz 3-6 (15+ lines daily) Complete ☐	• Revision: All Previous Surahs Complete ☐	• Revision: All Previous Duas Complete ☐	• Review All Islamic Studies Complete ☐
3-12 (36)	• Recitation Juz 3-6 (15+ lines daily) • Documentation: Quran Reading Rubric, Comprehensive Assessment Complete ☐	• Revision: All Previous Surahs • Documentation: Comprehensive Assessment Complete ☐	• Revision: All Previous Duas • Documentation: Comprehensive Assessment Complete ☐	• Review All Islamic Studies • Documentation: Comprehensive Assessment Complete ☐

Syllabus and Schedule

Grade _____ Teacher Name _____ Academic Year 20____ - 20____

Daily Schedule

Teacher, please complete the chart below in the beginning of the year to plan your class's daily schedule.

Subject	Monday	Tuesday	Wednesday	Thursday/(Friday)
Quran Reading and Tajwid				
Qaidah or Reading	minutes	minutes	minutes	minutes
Tajwid	minutes	minutes	minutes	minutes
Quran Memorization	minutes	minutes	minutes	minutes
Kalimah and Dua Memorization	minutes	minutes	minutes	minutes
Islamic Studies	minutes	minutes	minutes	minutes

Syllabus

Please complete the table below in the beginning of the year to plan the class syllabus. Please consult the curriculum to make sure all material from your grade level is covered.

Tri -Wk	Calendar Start Date	Quran Reading & Tajwid	Quran Memorization	Dua Memorization	Islamic Studies
1-1 (1)		• Complete Student Introductions and Fill Out Necessary Information in Class Register (Student Full Name, Parent Name, Phone Number, Medical Info) for Each Student • Conduct Motivational Sessions and Train Students in Class Rules and Etiquette. Review Student Code of Conduct. • Administer Placement Exam to All Students • Complete Maktab Assessments for All Students			
1-2 (2)		Complete ☐	Complete ☐	Complete ☐	Complete ☐
1-3 (3)		Complete ☐	Complete ☐	Complete ☐	Complete ☐
1-4 (4)		Complete ☐	Complete ☐	Complete ☐	Complete ☐

1-5 (5)	Complete ☐	Complete ☐	Complete ☐	Complete ☐
1-6 (6)	Complete ☐	Complete ☐	Complete ☐	Complete ☐
1-7 (7)	Complete ☐	Complete ☐	Complete ☐	Complete ☐
1-8 (8)	Complete ☐	Complete ☐	Complete ☐	Complete ☐
1-9 (9)	Complete ☐	Complete ☐	Complete ☐	Complete ☐
1-10 (10)	Complete ☐	Complete ☐	Complete ☐	Complete ☐
1-11 (11)	Complete ☐	Complete ☐	Complete ☐	Complete ☐
1-12 (12)	Complete ☐	Complete ☐	Complete ☐	Complete ☐
2-1 (13)	Complete ☐	Complete ☐	Complete ☐	Complete ☐

			Complete ☐
2-2 (14)	Complete ☐	Complete ☐	Complete ☐
2-3 (15)	Complete ☐	Complete ☐	Complete ☐
2-4 (16)	Complete ☐	Complete ☐	Complete ☐
2-5 (17)	Complete ☐	Complete ☐	Complete ☐
2-6 (18)	Complete ☐	Complete ☐	Complete ☐
2-7 (19)	Complete ☐	Complete ☐	Complete ☐
2-8 (20)	Complete ☐	Complete ☐	Complete ☐
2-9 (21)	Complete ☐	Complete ☐	Complete ☐
2-10 (22)	Complete ☐	Complete ☐	Complete ☐

		Complete ☐		Complete ☐		Complete ☐
(23)						
2-12		Complete ☐		Complete ☐		Complete ☐
(24)						
3-1		Complete ☐		Complete ☐		Complete ☐
(25)						
3-2		Complete ☐		Complete ☐		Complete ☐
(26)						
3-3		Complete ☐		Complete ☐		Complete ☐
(27)						
3-4		Complete ☐		Complete ☐		Complete ☐
(28)						
3-5		Complete ☐		Complete ☐		Complete ☐
(29)						
3-6		Complete ☐		Complete ☐		Complete ☐
(30)						
3-7		Complete ☐		Complete ☐		Complete ☐
(31)						

3-8 (32)	Complete ☐	Complete ☐	Complete ☐
3-9 (33)	Complete ☐	Complete ☐	Complete ☐
3-10 (34)	Complete ☐	Complete ☐	Complete ☐
3-11 (35)	Complete ☐	Complete ☐	Complete ☐
3-12 (36)	Complete ☐	Complete ☐	Complete ☐

Student Placement Worksheet

Student Name	Placement Criteria		Placement Grade				
	Age (Years)	Quran Fluency (Lines/3 min)	By Age	By Quran Fluency	By Islamic Studies (Aqidah)	By Islamic Studies (Fiqh)	Final Placement
1							
2							
3							
4							
5							
6							
7							
8							
9							
10							
11							
12							
13							
14							
15							

Age Placement

	Grade
Student is 5 years old in September	Qaidah
Student is 6 years old in September	1
Student is 7 years old in September	2
Student is 8 years old in September	3
Student is 9 years old in September	4
Student is 10 years old in September	5
Student is 11 years old in September	6
Student is 12 years old in September	7

Quran Fluency Placement

	Grade
Not able to read Quran	Qaidah
Read 1-5 lines in 3 minutes	1
Read 6-9 lines in 3 minutes	2
Read 10-13 lines in 3 minutes	3
Read 14-16 lines in 3 minutes	4 or above

Islamic Studies Placement

Utilize the Islamic Studies Placement Test.

Test each student:

1. With a copy of the Quran containing 15 lines per page.
2. On a portion of the Quran they have not recently read.
3. Having the student correct any mistake he/she makes.
2. Using Quran copy script (e.g. Madinah) student is used to.

Islamic Studies Placement Test

Name: _____ Age: _____ Date: _____

Aqaid (Beliefs)

Grade 1 1	A Muslim must believe in the following seven things. Fill in the blanks: 1. Allah 2. _____ 3. Allah' Revealed Books 4. _____ 5. The Last Day (Day of Judgment) 6. Fate (i.e. That Good and Bad is from Allah) 7. Life After Death
Grade 2 1	Muslims believe in the angels, who are a special creation of Allah. One of the angels is Jibrail (alaihissalam), who brought Allah's messages and books to the prophets. Circle names of some other angels below: a. Mikaeel (alaihis salam) b. Adam (alaihis salam) c. Israfil (alaihis salam) d. Iblis
Grade 2 2	Name the four major books revealed to the prophets:
Grade 3 1	Name some of the messengers of Allah:
Grade 3 2	Who was the last messenger that was sent by Allah?
Grade 4 1	What are some of the signs of the Day of Judgment?
Grade 4 2	On the Day of Judgment, there will be a bridge. What is the name of this bridge, and why will people have to cross it?
Grade 4 3	Who is the Dajjal? How will he look like? Will he be good or evil?

Fiqh (Practice)

Grade 1 1	List the five pillars of Islam: 1. 2. 3. 4. 5.
Grade 1 2	How do you make wudu? List the steps and the body parts that need to be washed.
Grade 2 1	What are the things that break one's wudu (i.e. nawaqid of wudu)?
Grade 2 2	What is tayammum?
Grade 3 1	What is ghusl? What are the faraid (requirements) of ghusl?
Grade 3 2	How many rakats are there in the fardh of each of the five prayers (salah)? Fajr: _____ Zuhr: _____ Asr: _____ Maghrib: _____ Isha: _____
Grade 4 1	When can one wipe over khuffain (leather socks) during wudu?
Grade 4 2	What is sajdah sahw, and when would one peform it?

Student Code of Conduct

Objective

Development of good character, conduct, and morals is a main objective of our religion Islam. Allah has stressed the importance of good character, and our Prophet Muhammad (صلى الله عليه وسلم) was a model of good character.

أَكْمَلُ المؤْمِنِينَ إِيمَانًا أَحْسَنُهُمْ خُلُقًا (رواه أحمد)

The believers most complete in their faith are those that are best in their character.

The student code of conduct aims to teach students good character. This will promote a safe and healthy learning environment at our school.

Student Conduct

The following generally describes good student behavior.

1. Student treats others with courtesy and respect, both verbally and physically. This includes other students. It also includes teachers, staff, and others in the masjid.

2. Student follows the directions of his/her teachers and other teachers/staff during class time, during prayers, and after class dismissal.

3. Student pays attention to the teacher and actively participates in class activities. This promotes a distraction free learning environment and affords due respect to religious knowledge.

4. Student respects the property of others. This includes the property of other students, the teacher, and the masjid.

5. Student honors the sanctity of the masjid and of prayer. While in the prayer hall waiting for prayer, and after prayer has been completed, student focuses on praying the sunnah prayers, remembering Allah (making *zikr*), or sitting quietly.

6. Student observes proper grooming which includes wearing a clean, loose, picture free, full sleeve dress that covers the body. Boys must wear a cap, and girls must wear a hijab. Students are encouraged to wear ironed clothes without stains or tears. Perfumes, if applied, must be light. Sportswear is not allowed. Students must observe hygiene (including trimming of hairs and nails).

7. Student is punctual and observes discipline in his or her time.

Incentives and Corrective Action

Teachers and staff are responsible for teaching students about good conduct, modeling it themselves, promoting it in practice, and when necessary, taking corrective action against violations of this standard.

From time to time, teachers will provide incentives to students that include rewards for excellence in learning and good behavior. These may include weekly incentives or rewards on specific occasions. Incentives are a positive and motivational means for promoting good conduct.

If a student violates the code of conduct outlined above, corrective measures will be implemented.

Types of Behavioral Violations

Conduct and actions which are contrary to the good student behavior outlined in the Student Conduct section above are considered behavioral violations. The following are Type 1 violations (Behavioral Violations):

1. Not following the teacher's directions and general class rules.
2. Making fun of, taunting, or being rude to fellow students.
3. Misbehaving during prayer times in the prayer hall (i.e. right before and after the congregational prayer, while waiting for prayer, and during sunnah prayers).
4. Excessiveness roughness during play, especially when it hurts others.
5. Wearing clothes to school that smell or are unclean (except with a valid reason) or are

Type 1 violations (Behavioral Violations) may lead to one of the following disciplinary actions at the discretion of the teacher or staff member. These may be recorded in the student's progress book or teacher's records, but no special notice will be sent home to parents.

- The optional break will be forfeited up to 3 days.
- Student will not be allowed to participate in a regular weekly or monthly incentive or treat.
- Student will be required to sit in a special quiet area or seat
- Student will be required to stand up and/or face the wall for up to 30 minutes.
- Teacher at his/her discretion will implement any other minor, non-physical disciplinary measure.

The following are more severe Type 2 violations (Severe Behavioral Violations).

1. Fighting with, beating, or otherwise physically harming a fellow student (or others at school)
2. Use of vulgar language such as swear words.
3. Intentionally damaging or stealing others' property including that of the school
4. Rude behavior or insubordination to the teacher
5. Taunting others based on race, color, national origin, or language
6. Lewd and inappropriate dressing (which does not cover the *'awrah*)
7. Possessing items prohibited in school (dangerous items/substances, weapons, lewd/vulgar material)
8. Cheating on a test or exam

These violations are taken more seriously. In case of any Type 2 violation, a Notice of Behavioral Violation must be sent home to be signed by the parent and returned. Additionally, any one of the disciplinary actions above, or one of following additional disciplinary actions, may be taken. (Please also not that on the third serious Type 2 violation within an academic year, a student may be suspended.)

- The optional break will be forfeited up to 5 days.
- Student will be required to serve after school detention.

Reporting

Students and parents are encouraged to report any incidences and violations of the student conduct to the teacher or to the principal. The teacher or principal will ascertain the facts and determine corrective action. Please note that violations will be punishable when ascertained by reliable witnesses, such as an adult or multiple mature students.

Notice of Behavioral Violation

Dear Parent/Guardian,

Assalamu alaikum. We regret to inform you that on _____ (date) at _____ (time), your child _____ committed the following severe (Type 2) violation of our Code of Conduct for students:

- ❑ Fighting with, beating, or otherwise physically harming a fellow student (or others at school)
- ❑ Use of vulgar language such as swear words
- ❑ Intentionally damaging or stealing others' property including that of the school
- ❑ Rude behavior or insubordination to the teacher
- ❑ Taunting others based on race, color, national origin, or language
- ❑ Lewd and inappropriate dressing (which does not cover the *'awrah*)
- ❑ Possessing items prohibited in school (dangerous items/substances, weapons, lewd/vulgar material)
- ❑ Cheating on a test or exam

This type of violation is considered a very severe behavioral offence and is taken seriously at our school. We request you to have a conversation with your child about the seriousness of this offence and how it must be avoided in the future. This is the ❑ 1st ❑ 2nd ❑ 3rd ❑ _____ time a serious (Type 2) offence has been committed this year. (Please note that we normally do not report less serious Type 1 offences to parents.) As such, the following disciplinary action will be taken:

- ❑ The optional break will be taken away for the following days: _____
- ❑ Student must serve after school detention on the following days and times: _____
- ❑ Student will be suspended from school on the following days: _____
- ❑ Other disciplinary action: _____

Please note that on the third such serious Type 2 offence within an academic year, students are subject to suspension from school.

Additional Comments: _____

_____

_____

Parents are required to sign this note below and return it the next day to the teacher.

_____   _____
Teacher(s) or Principal Signature   Date

I acknowledge that I have read this letter and have discussed this behavioral offence with my child.

_____   _____
Parent Signature   Date

Copyright © Masjid Uthman (Uthman Academy, Uthman Seminary)

Student Notes

Student Name
_____
Date
Date
Date
Date

Student Name
_____
Date
Date
Date
Date

Student Notes

Student Name
_____
Date:
Date:
Date:

Student Name
_____
Date:
Date:
Date:

Student Notes

Student Name
_____
Date:
Date:
Date:
Date:

Student Name
_____
Date:
Date:
Date:
Date:

Student Notes

Student Name
_____
Date:
Date:
Date:
Date:

Student Name
_____
Date:
Date:
Date:
Date:

Student Notes

Student Name
_____

Date

Date

Date

Date

Student Name
_____

Date

Date

Date

Date

Student Notes

Student Name
_____
Date
Date
Date
Date

Student Name
_____
Date
Date
Date
Date

My Meeting Notes

Meeting Date

_____ / _____ / _____

Updates / Decisions:

My Action Items:
1.

2.

3.

Meeting Date

_____ / _____ / _____

Updates / Decisions:

My Action Items:
1.

2.

3.

My Meeting Notes

Meeting Date

____ / ____ / ____

Updates / Decisions:

My Action Items:
1.

2.

3.

Meeting Date

____ / ____ / ____

Updates / Decisions:

My Action Items:
1.

2.

3.

My Meeting Notes

Meeting Date
　　____ / ____ / ____

Updates / Decisions:

My Action Items:
1.

2.

3.

Meeting Date
　　____ / ____ / ____

Updates / Decisions:

My Action Items:
1.

2.

3.

My Meeting Notes

Meeting Date
     ____ / ____ / ____

Updates / Decisions:

My Action Items:
1.

2.

3.

Meeting Date
     ____ / ____ / ____

Updates / Decisions:

My Action Items:
1.

2.

3.

My Meeting Notes

Meeting Date
       ____ / ____ / ____

Updates / Decisions:

My Action Items:
1.

2.

3.

Meeting Date
       ____ / ____ / ____

Updates / Decisions:

My Action Items:
1.

2.

3.

My Meeting Notes

Meeting Date
____ / ____ / ____

Updates / Decisions:

My Action Items:
1.

2.

3.

Meeting Date
____ / ____ / ____

Updates / Decisions:

My Action Items:
1.

2.

3.

Student Rotational Duties

Duty	Assigned Students		
	Trimester 1	Trimester 2	Trimester 3
1 After Class: Throw Away Trash Lying in Halls/Masjid/Class Areas	Student 1 Name Student 2 Name	Student 1 Name Student 2 Name	Student 1 Name Student 2 Name
2 After Lunch: Clean Areas That Apply to Lunchroom Areas	Student 1 Name Student 2 Name	Student 1 Name Student 2 Name	Student 1 Name Student 2 Name
3 After Lunch: Restore Chairs/Desks	Student 1 Name Student 2 Name	Student 1 Name Student 2 Name	Student 1 Name Student 2 Name
4 After Class: Pat Away Teacher Desk	Student 1 Name Student 2 Name	Student 1 Name Student 2 Name	Student 1 Name Student 2 Name
5 Clean Board, Organize Art (pm)	Student 1 Name Student 2 Name	Student 1 Name Student 2 Name	Student 1 Name Student 2 Name
6			
7			
8			
9			
10			

Use this chart to assign students to specific duties every trimester/semester. Teachers should monitor and inspect completion of these duties. Assignment of duties will build student character and the spirit of service and civic responsibility (خدمة). It will also provide valuable assistance in facility maintenance. Suggested, common duties have been included in the table, but the space in the table may be overwritten.

Teacher Rotational Duties

Duty	Teacher(s)
Class Starts: Open Facility Doors, Monitor Student Arrivals, Setup Lunches Etc.	Teacher Name
Class Starts: Inspect Shoe Area, Bag Area for Proper Student Placement of Shoes/Bags	Teacher Name
After Class: Inspect Student Cleanup	Teacher Name
After Class: Monitor Student Dismissal	Teacher Name
After Class: Supervise Students Picked Up Late on the Following Days:	Teacher Name
After Class: Supervise Students Picked Up Late on the Following Days:	Teacher Name
After Class: Supervise Students Picked Up Late on the Following Days:	Teacher Name
After Class: Supervise Students Picked Up Late on the Following Days:	Teacher Name
Plan Special Events: Parent Workshop, Convocation	Teacher Name
Plan/Purchase Student Treats and Incentive Items	Teacher Name
Plan Class Parties (Eid Parties, Pre-Break Parties, Farewell Parties)	Teacher Name

Teacher Rotational Duties are those duties typically assisgned to a teacher (rather than a school administrator or principal). Suggested duties are included in grey, but these can be overwritten based on needs of the school. When there are multiple teachers but no full time management/administration, this chart will be useful to make sure all activities are executed efficiently.

Student Medical Info

Student Full Name	Medical Needs (Allergies, Phsychological, Special Needs, Disabilities)
1	
2	
3	
4	
5	
6	
7	
8	
9	
10	
11	
12	
13	
14	
15	
16	
17	

Fee Tracker (Admin Use)

Student Full Name   **Tuition and Fees** (Paid / Financial Assistance)

	Initial												
Standard Fee	$	$	$	$	$	$	$	$	$	$	$	$	$
Sibling Discount Fee	$	$	$	$	$	$	$	$	$	$	$	$	$
1													
2													
3													
4													
5													
6													
7													
8													
9													
10													
11													
12													
13													
14													
15													
16													
17													
All Students Up to Date (✔)													

NA Fee not applicable in this period.

Made in the USA
Las Vegas, NV
08 September 2024